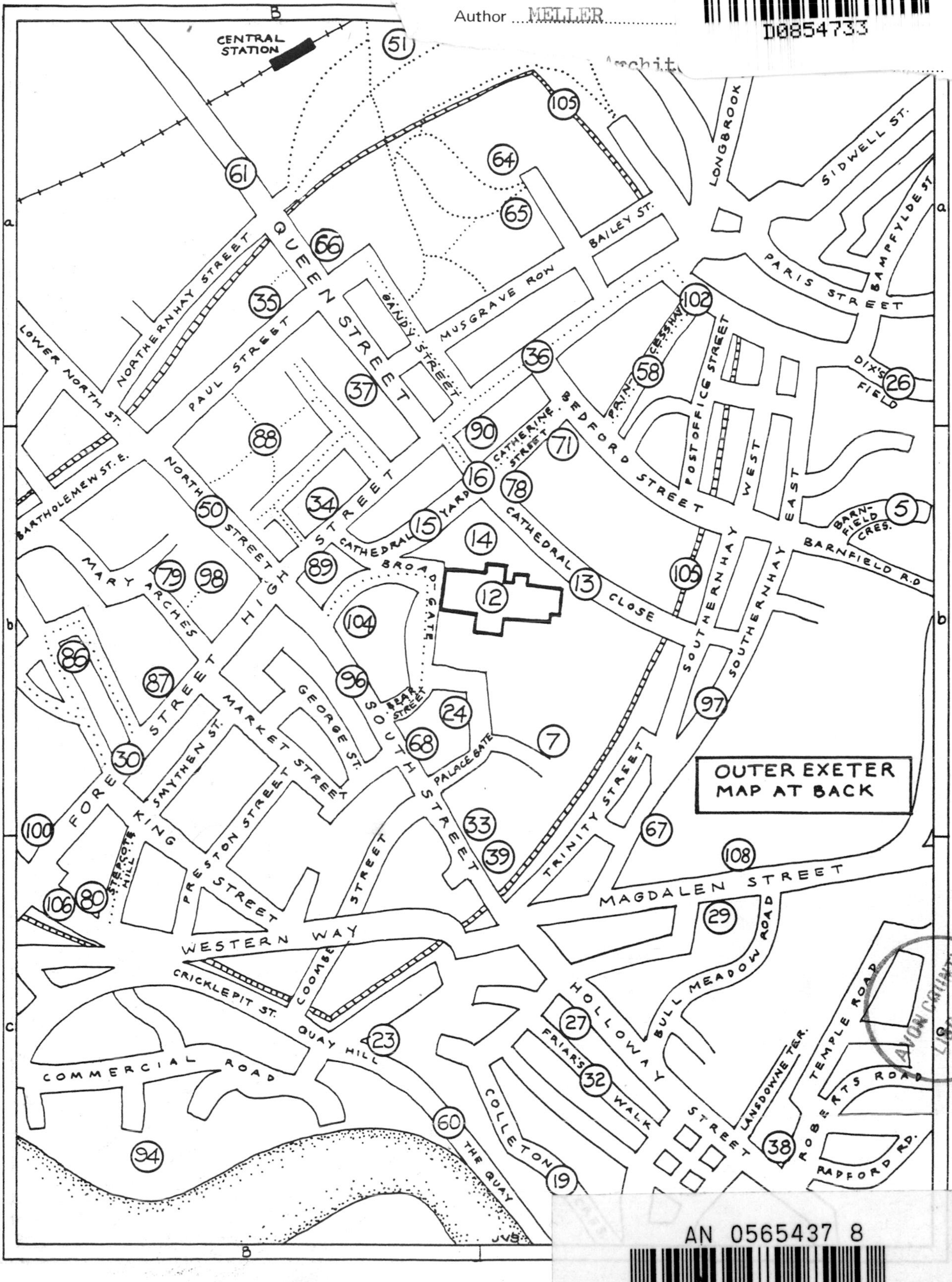

CENTRAL STATION

QUEEN STREET
NORTHERNHAY STREET
LOWER NORTH ST.
PAUL STREET
BARTHOLEMEW ST. E.
NORTH STREET
MARY ARCHES
HIGH STREET
FORE STREET
SMYTHEN ST.
MARKET STREET
GEORGE ST.
KING STREET
STEPCOTE HILL
PRESTON STREET
SANDY STREET
MUSGRAVE ROW
BAILEY ST.
LONGBROOK
SIDWELL ST.
BAMPFYLDE ST.
PARIS STREET
DIX'S FIELD
PRINCESSHAY
POST OFFICE STREET
BEDFORD STREET
CATHERINE STREET
CATHEDRAL YARD
CATHEDRAL CLOSE
BROAD GATE
SOUTHERNHAY WEST
SOUTHERNHAY EAST
BARNFIELD CRES.
BARNFIELD RD
BEAR STREET
PALACE GATE
SOUTH STREET
TRINITY STREET
MAGDALEN STREET
WESTERN WAY
COOMBE STREET
CRICKLEPIT ST.
QUAY HILL
COMMERCIAL ROAD
THE QUAY
COLLETON
FRIAR'S WALK
HOLLOWAY STREET
BULL MEADOW ROAD
LANSDOWNE TER.
TEMPLE ROAD
ROBERTS ROAD
RADFORD RD.

OUTER EXETER MAP AT BACK

JVS

EXETER ARCHITECTURE

No. 10, Cathedral Close

EXETER ARCHITECTURE

Hugh Meller

Phillimore

1989

Published by
PHILLIMORE & CO. LTD.,
Shopwyke Hall, Chichester, Sussex

ISBN 0 85033 693 7

Printed and bound in Great Britain by
RICHARD CLAY LTD.,
Bungay, Suffolk

Contents

List of Illustrations

Frontispiece: *No. 10, Cathedral Close*

Illustration Acknowledgements

The author wishes to express his gratitude to the Royal Albert Memorial Museum for permission to reproduce illustrations nos. 93 & 109.

Foreword

The main difficulty encountered whilst writing this book was deciding what to exclude. Of the buildings recognised by Act of Parliament as being of special architectural or historic interest, all those listed Grade I (13 at the time of writing) and nearly all Grade II*(67) are here. There remain, however, over 700 Grade II listed buildings in Exeter and that was too many for a book that is not intended to be exhaustive but rather a selection of representative buildings, some of which are not listed at all. Inevitably where a choice was necessary those rejected tended to be on the outskirts of the city.

There are just over one hundred individual entries but, because many of them deal with more than one building, approximately two hundred of the finest buildings in Exeter are described. I am aware that many others were candidates for inclusion: non-conformist churches, old industrial sites, 17th-century farm buildings, 18th-century terraces and 19th-century houses. I can only apologise to readers who discover that favourite buildings of theirs are missing and hope that they may be satisfied with the alternatives.

The geographical area covered is the city and its suburbs except Topsham which deserves a book to itself. All standing structures and excavated buildings from the Roman Conquest to the present day are within the brief, as are street and park sculptures. I have visited all those described and, where it was relevant, managed to see inside all save one. I am very grateful to those who showed me round and answered questions. There are also special thanks due to Tiggy Ruthven and Chris Vile who took a number of the photographs, Jane Schofield who drew the map and read and checked the typescript, and Miriam Wakefield, Glen Bauer and Ann Bartholomew who typed much of the manuscript.

Finally, as a comparative newcomer to Devon, I cannot claim an unrivalled knowledge of Exeter's architectural history; mistakes will be unavoidable, and I will be glad to hear of any corrections or additions that readers care to make.

H.M.
Bradninch 1989

Introduction

Exeter, it must be admitted, is no longer a city with obvious architectural riches. True, there is the Cathedral, one of the finest 13th-century churches in the country, and the Guildhall, a civic building of unrivalled antiquity, but then what? There are no major parish churches as one finds in, say, Norwich or York, there are no great industrial monuments as in Bristol and farther north and there are few big names among the architects who practised here, certainly none of national importance until the 19th century. The reasons must be partly due to geographical isolation until the railway reached the city in 1844, partly economic decline after the 18th century and partly the calamitous disaster of the Blitz which destroyed or seriously damaged 4,200 houses, 640 commercial buildings and nine churches. This appalling destruction reduced Exeter's medieval heart to rubble and the bleak new buildings fail to provide a focus or recapture the spirit of a regional capital as in Taunton, Bristol, Cardiff or even Plymouth. Often Exeter's best buildings are found in unexpected places – a medieval convent in a housing estate, a church squashed into a shopping centre, parts of the old city walls bordering car parks, a Tudor house overwhelmed by factories, a medieval bridge surrounded by new roads and early 19th-century terraces down private drives. The buildings are there but hidden, although, once unravelled from the later veneer, their antiquity is undeniable.

There has been human habitation in Exeter for over two thousand years but the history of the city becomes clear only after the Roman occupation in about A.D. 50. During the next 350 years, the Romans built a town within a rectangle of stone walls in which the main streets were laid out in the traditional grid plan. The lines of these remain, and the walls still reveal Roman remnants dating from about A.D. 200, which are now the oldest standing structures in the city.

During the fifth century the Romans withdrew from Britain and for the next 300 years nothing is known about Exeter and only a few traces of Saxon work in the central parish churches constitute physical evidence of the following 300, although by 1066 it had become one of the biggest towns in England.

The Normans captured Exeter in 1068 and left their indelible mark: a cathedral and Rougemont castle, of which the transept towers and the gatehouse, respectively, remain. They had also built 32 churches by the end of the 12th century in a city that ranked fourth in size after London, York and Winchester. The cloth and wine trade flourished, the port was busy and one of the earliest and longest stone bridges in the country was built over the river Exe.

During the 13th century a new project was started: rebuilding the cathedral from end to end in the new Decorated style. It was a task that took 100 years to complete. Houses of that date do not survive; the earliest examples in Exeter are 15th century, in West Street, High Street, North Street and Catherine Street. They are often separated by party walls of Heavitree stone, that most distinctive of local building materials first quarried at the end of the 14th century.

By the 16th century Devon's prominent role in the nation's woollen industry generated a rich merchant class in Exeter which expressed itself in fabulous gabled houses, like those in the High Street, and by beautifying the 14th-century Guildhall with the addition of a columned porch. The canal too was dug in the 1560s to improve the port facilities.

The 17th century was an eventful one for Exeter. The cloth trade declined and during the Civil War and its aftermath the royalist city underwent a siege and military occupation from which it did not fully recover until the end of the century. This period is now known as the Golden Age of Exeter, exemplified in architecture by the Customs House of 1681, one of the city's earliest brick buildings fitted inside with three decorative ceilings, the finest in Exeter to illustrate this west country plasterwork speciality. Celia Fiennes visited in 1698 and described Exeter as 'a town very well built. The streets are well pitched, spacious, noble streets' comparable with London. It was the fifth largest town in England whose wealth was still based on the wool trade.

Prosperity continued into the 18th century witnessed by the creation of several large public buildings: the hospital (1743), the synagogue (1763), the assembly rooms (now the *Clarence Hotel*) (1769), the county prison (1790), banks and chapels. The names of local architect/builders like John Brown, the Hooper family, Matthew Nosworthy and Robert Stribling become familiar and towards the end of the century the first of many elegant Regency terraces had been built at Bedford Circus (1773), Barnfield Crescent (1792) and Southernhay (1792). The same style of terrace, sometimes with distinctive Coade stone voussoirs around the doors and generally with intricate ironwork balconies, continued to be built into the 19th century although by the third decade landscaped villas like Pennsylvania Park were the fashion.

One of the most productive periods in Exeter's architectural history occurred during the short reign of William IV (1830-37) when Dymond and Fowler's masterpiece, the neo-Greek Higher Market was begun, the Iron Bridge spanned the Longbrook valley and two of the largest warehouses yet seen in Britain were built on the quay. Richard Ford, writing in 1834, enthused over his new home, 'This Exeter is quite a Capital, abounding in all that London has, except its fog and smoke'. It was a suitably ambitious introduction to the frenetic building activity of the Victorian era.

Acres of new brick terrace houses extending far into the suburbs constituted the most obvious change and with them rose the amenities necessary to service their inhabitants: new almshouses, churches, hospitals, pubs, schools, shops and new building types like cemeteries and railway stations. Building techniques too were being developed and mass produced materials brought in by rail to supersede the local stone and slate. (Old cob walls can occasionally be found in central Exeter but the last thatched roof was apparently removed in 1882.) Civic pride and self-awareness inspired the city to build the museum (1885) and university (1900). Parks and streets were furnished with statues and monuments, parish churches and the cathedral were expensively restored and for the first time London architects were employed: William Butterfield at Exeter School, Gilbert Scott and J. L. Pearson in the cathedral, Rhode Hawkins at St Michael's, Dinham Road, Leonard Stokes at the Sacred Heart Church and W. D. Caroë at St David's. Most daring of all was the employment of Paul Cottancin, a French pioneer of reinforced concrete, who engineered the construction, in 1902, of Sidwell Street Methodist church dome.

Cottancin went bankrupt in the process and it was an ill omen that seems to have dogged Exeter throughout the 20th century. In 1898 the first car drove into town, 20 years later 1,300 driving licences had been issued and street widening schemes bulldozed old houses in their way. In the 1930s much of the West Quarter was demolished but that was only a prelude to the Blitz during the spring of 1942. On the night of 3-4 May, 75 tons of bombs fell in one and a half hours, devastating High Street, Sidwell Street, Fore Street, Southernhay, South Street, Paris Street, Newtown and St Leonards, among others. One fifth of the city's buildings were destroyed.

In 1945 a town planner, Thomas Sharp, was engaged to devise a plan for the city's renewal. It was a tremendous challenge to which, in theory at least, he offered a suitable solution. 'The way to rebuild a city like this is in sympathetic, not ruthless renewal.

Sympathetic planning in such a case lies in the observance of scale and in the creation of intimate rather than monumental forms . . .' But it was not to be. Sharp's plans for the most part were overruled as the city's shopkeepers battled with the council at a public enquiry in 1946. The council sought powers of compulsory purchase over the bomb sites so it could implement a 'Central Areas Reconstruction Plan', the shopkeepers objected in favour of the *status quo*. They lost and the bland rebuilding and depredations of the 1950s and '60s began. The result was a tragedy summed up in the April 1966 edition of *Devon Life* by Rodney Hallworth: 'The heart of Exeter is dead. Because the men and women entrusted to forge its future and reshape its centre blasted by war have quarrelled the once proud city is now a shambles of ghost streets and stricken development'. This is harsh criticism and not without justification but in the last 10 years a fresh initiative has at last emerged. In 1979 the prizewinning Shilhay housing estate was designed in the spirit of Sharp's words whilst just down river the redevelopment of the quay area is a revelation. Perhaps, with luck, the example set in this, the historic economic heart of Exeter, will encourage an architectural renaissance to spread.

Rougemont Castle, Exeter

THE ATWILL/GRENDON ALMSHOUSES, GRENDON ROAD

Architecturally these are perhaps the most distinguished pair of Exeter's almshouses which, although looking similar, were in fact built in two phases, the Grendon range to the south in 1880, the Atwill in 1892. Robert Best of Exeter was architect for both.

The Grendon range, in Pocombe stone, replaced almshouses known as 'The Ten Cells' of Preston Street, founded in 1406 by Simon Grendon, a mayor of Exeter. The softer Heavitree stone Atwill range, with its detail smudged by weathering, also replaces an earlier group, founded in Northernhay by Lawrence Atwill in 1588, but swallowed up by inner-city development.

The architectural style is a stately Elizabethan: tall brick chimneystacks above steep gables and generous porches. Lawns surround both ranges which contain 24 apartments in all. There is a marked contrast between these dignified buildings and the neighbouring blocks of ugly modern flats.

THE ATWILL/PALMER ALMSHOUSES, NEW NORTH ROAD

Lawrence Atwill made his fortune as a skinner in London, but he never forgot that Exeter was his birthplace. On his death in 1588 his will directed that almshouses should be endowed for the benefit of 24 poor persons aged over 60 who had lived in the city for 10 years. This was done, first in Northernhay Street, and moving in 1839 to the present site as the endowment prospered. In 1883 four of the dwellings became the responsibility of the Palmer Charity, originally founded in 1487.

The houses are built of Pocombe stone as three groups of semi-detached villas in the Tudor style that was popular in the early 19th century. The roofs are gabled and the mullioned windows dressed in Bath stone to give a convincing impression of antiquity. Surrounding them are lawns and yew trees. At the back, new bathrooms and kitchens have been added, but the old stone privies survive as potting sheds.

BARING CRESCENT

The best of Exeter's domestic architecture was built 30 years before and after 1800. The process started with the set piece brick terraces of Southernhay, Barnfield Crescent and Bedford Circus, and ended 60 years later with the stuccoed villas of Mont le Grand. Heavitree and St Leonards, on the east of the city, were especially popular suburbs during the later years; a contemporary directory reported in 1828 that Heavitree 'has, within the last few years, felt extensively the exhilarating hand of improvement. The vast number of genteel houses and villas recently erected here far exceed our limits of description'. Typical of these, built on the old Baring Estate, was Baring Crescent.

The developer was a local man, John Brown, who went on to build Pennsylvania Crescent. Compared with the latter these houses are very austere, but the principle is the same – a semi-circular group of 12 detached villas enjoying their own communal pleasure ground to the front. They comprise a basement, which contained a kitchen, scullery,

1. Atwill/Grendon Almshouses, Heavitree Road.

2. Atwill/Palmer Almshouses, New North Road.

housekeeper's room, pantry, beer and wine cellars, a piano-nobile above set behind a balcony of iron railings, containing a dining room, drawing room, breakfast room and butler's pantry, and on the two floors above a second drawing room and eight bedrooms. In 1818, when the foundation stone was laid, they were described, surprisingly, only as 'superior cottages'! Today such accommodation sounds vast, with the inevitable result that they have been converted for office and institutional use.

Changes began with the Victorians and their enthusiasm for plate glass and bay windows, which look out of place on flat fronted classical facades. Two houses have disappeared entirely, the rest suffer from a variety of insensitive alterations and additions, virulent 20th-century paint colours and a disastrous invasion of cars, which has caused several back gardens to be tarmacadamed and a rash of 'no parking' signs and obstructions just about everywhere else.

3. Baring Crescent.

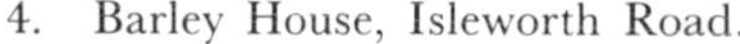

4. Barley House, Isleworth Road.

BARLEY HOUSE, ISLEWORTH ROAD

Exwick is surely the most depressing of Exeter's suburbs. Dreary streets of 20th-century houses sprawl up the western side of the Exe Valley, creating an architectural desert with few redeeming features. Barley House is a rare exception, once served by a carriage drive that is now Isleworth Road.

There has been more than one house on this site, whose commanding view of the city attracted a parliamentary garrison during the Civil War. In the 18th century John Pinnock lived here, but the style of the present building is chastely classical, which dates it to the early 19th century when it was re-built by Charles Collyns, an Exeter banker.

It is a stuccoed two-storey five-bay house, with only a Doric portico to break up a severely plain facade. Inside there is a central curving staircase with cast-iron honeysuckle (*anthemion*) banisters and several rooms with richly-decorated plaster ceilings. It sounds inviting, but in 1939 the house was bought for the county's library services and today the interiors are difficult to appreciate as they have been swamped with bookcases and all the paraphernalia of a busy office. It is a sad irony that an educational establishment like this should so dismally fail to set an example by using the building in such an insensitive way.

In 1969 a new two-storey brick extension was linked to one side. It won a Civic Trust award, which is surprising as the building is totally unremarkable.

5. Barnfield Crescent.

BARNFIELD CRESCENT

Before the 19th century, and particularly the foundation of the R.I.B.A. in 1837, builders, speculators and architects were often one and the same man. Typical was Matthew Nosworthy (1750-1831), a native of Widecombe imbued with 'great ingenuity and perseverance' who was responsible for four of the finest Regency terraces in Exeter.

The Crescent was his second major venture, planned fashionably in the round like the Circus at Bath which had set the pace in the 1750s, modelled on the Roman Colosseum. Exeter had followed with Robert Stribling's speculative Bedford Circus (damaged in the Blitz and since pulled down), begun 20 years later and still being built when Nosworthy signed the contract for building 'at least 27 houses' in Barnfield Crescent in 1792. Like many speculative developments progress was laboriously slow, dependent on completing the sale of one house before investing in the next. Eventually after 14 years Nosworthy had built only five houses (another was added in 1840), probably rather less than one quadrant of his Circus plan, and the project ended, but despite that the completed fragment is impressive.

The houses are built on a larger scale than Bedford Circus, too large now to be single domestic units, but before they inevitably succumbed to office use, Richardson and Gill, writing in 1924, captured their essence: 'The terrace has the merit of rich simplicity; the front consists of four ranges of windows, the lower being arcuated with double rims. Jalousies, elegant balconettes of wrought iron and a delicately trellised verandah combine to produce a picture of persuasive and refined charm'.

THE BARRACKS, HOWELL ROAD, AND BARRACK ROAD

Unless one has business with the army, Pennsylvania barracks are difficult to see because the old brick buildings face inwards across a parade ground and the approach is obscured by a jumble of huts and offices. The original buildings were designed for cavalry, 'sufficiently capacious for about 200 horses', and date from 1792 when the threat of a Napoleonic invasion was very real.

On the west side are two accommodation blocks and opposite, the stables and riding school, with a row of eight arched openings for the horses and above, supported on the slenderest iron columns, an iron balustraded balcony providing access to the grooms' quarters. The architect is unknown. In 1867 the red brick pedimented wing with its central clock tower filled the north side and in 1875 a terrace of houses, now outside the west perimeter of the barracks, repeated the balcony technique to create two levels of married quarters.

The barracks were latterly used by the Devon Regiment which moved out in 1948 to the former Artillery barracks in Barrack Road where there is a vast parade ground, but only one building of note – a long brick block on the north side dated 1804. The centrepiece is five bays wide surmounted by a pediment which carries an enormous Georgian royal coat of arms in Coade stone and above that an equally heavyweight clock tower. There is nothing remarkable inside and at the time of writing the building is no longer a barracks, but awaits a new use.

THE BISHOP'S PALACE, PALACE GATE

Some episcopal palaces, like Durham, Wells and Winchester, are of great architectural importance and still reflect the enormous wealth and power of their ecclesiastical builders, but this is no longer so at Exeter where extensive alterations by numerous bishops have left only sterile fragments of a great medieval house.

The 14th-century gatehouse is one of the fragments, modernised in the 18th century and

6. The Barracks, Howell Road.

7. Bishop's Palace Gatehouse, Palace Gate.

again by William Butterfield in 1875, when the stone mullioned windows were inserted leaving only two original slit openings. Beyond it spread the palace gardens enclosed by the old city walls and east end of the cathedral itself. Here there is ample space among the flower borders to pitch marquees for garden parties or cricket nets for the choir school in an unmistakable English setting, but to enter the palace after this is an anti-climax. Only the cavernous 14th-century porch, and 13th-century south door richly framed by colonnettes, stiff leaf capitals and an exotic zig-zag decorated arch, are of palatial size.

The main block of the existing palace is now three storeyed under an 18th-century twin-gable roof. Originally this was the 13th-century great hall, measuring about 75 feet by 42 feet, but more and more rooms have been carved from it so that few clues to its origin survive. The most thorough change occurred in 1848 when Ewan Christian (1814-95), architect to the Ecclesiastical Commissioners, reduced the size of the palace and re-fashioned the remains using the neo-Tudor style now evident in the exterior. In his 1932 history of the palace, John Chanter described the result as, 'A most uncomfortable and badly planned house that man ever conceived, utterly devoid of any sanitary arrangement, the lighting and ventilation being extremely bad'.

Not surprisingly most bishops thereafter lived elsewhere until in 1948 the palace was modernised once again and almost all its surviving old features were obliterated. The three openings (now glazed) of the screens passage and an embedded timber column that once supported an aisle of the great hall survive, just, but the rest is left to the imagination. In an otherwise featureless drawing room, a baronial-sized chimney piece looks isolated.

It was originally installed by Bishop Courtney (1478-87) in the west wing, but it has been re-positioned twice, most recently in 1952 when the heraldic decoration was repainted. (Its fame was such that when the great hall of the Courtney home at Powderham was remodelled by Charles Fowler in 1848 he copied it.) The present dining room, once the library, is another dour room, cheered up by the patchwork of heraldic glass in a large bay window, moved here in the 19th century from a house in Cathedral Yard (a water-colour in the Devon and Exeter Institution illustrates it in its original position), and opposite, a gothic fireplace by Ewan Christian.

There is little more to be said. The west wing is now used for offices and the Cathedral library. A medieval octagonal staircase tower remains at one end, but the interior is spartan 1950s. Linked to this building is the 13th-century bishop's chapel. The three fine lancet windows at the east end were repaired by Butterfield, who restored the chapel in 1878 and created the ante-chapel. Today it is no longer used for worship and the High Victorian decoration has been painted over. It is a sad end to a sad building. It can only be a matter of time before it is once and for all decided that the palace does not make a comfortable home and further conversion to a more practical purpose seems inevitable. Architecturally this will be no great loss.

BLESSED SACRAMENT CHURCH, HEAVITREE ROAD

An alien Roman character distinguishes this 1930s' church from any other in Exeter. The red brick exterior with Portland stone dressings is embellished with sculpture either side of the green marble columned portico, a western peripteral apse and an eastern tower which houses a four-ton bell that escaped Blitz damage when the tower itself suffered and was reduced to half its size. The cost of the building was borne by two devout Torquay ladies, and must have been considerable as some of the materials used were as unusual as the architectural style.

The church has an unexpectedly traditional basilica plan with walls painted in discreet white and grey which admirably sets off the exotic marbles of the columns and baptistry

8. Blessed Sacrament church, Heavitree Road.

9. Bowhill, Dunsford Road.

furnishings. The arching is in brèche violette (a composite stone), and the baldacchino supported by seven columns of Italian cipollino (a marble interfoliated with veins of talc, mica, quartz etc.). The altar table is in green onyx. Happily the interior is free of tawdry trappings so that these unusual materials are seen to advantage.

BOWHILL, DUNSFORD ROAD

Along with some houses in the Close, Bowhill ranks amongst the finest of Exeter's dwindling number of surviving medieval houses and it is now receiving a long overdue restoration. By the time this is complete English Heritage will have spent £600,000's worth of public money on the house over a period of 12 years, an indication of its importance.

Bowhill appears to date from the mid-15th century and may have been built by Richard Holland, M.P. (*c*.1385-1450), whose family were related to the Dukes of Exeter and which had owned property on this site since the 13th century. The house now comprises three wings, but there is evidence of a fourth, which suggests an original courtyard plan. The shortest wing, to the west, housed the kitchen, remarkable for a ceiling densely supported by chamfered joists, and a large fireplace arch built of light volcanic blocks. These are notched in such a way that each is joggled into position for extra strength. To one side is the opening for a bread oven.

As was customary by the early 15th century, the kitchen was separated from the hall by another wing to the south, running parallel to Dunsford Road, which housed the butteries, the parlour and two large rooms above. The parlour has a moulded cross-beamed ceiling, but in the solar above there is an open roof of four bays with the distinctive Exeter feature of an intermediate truss added between the main arch braces, each embellished with a leaf carved boss on the point of the lower cusp. The hall roof in the east wing is similar, but without the carved bosses, and both are peculiar in having a small upper coving above the apex of the arch braced timbers, another Exeter speciality (*see* p. 43).

The hall has a traditional plank and muntin screens passage at its south end, a fireplace and four large rectangular windows each divided by a mullion and transom into four foil-headed lights. There is an upper room at its far end, but, as with the solar above the parlour, the access staircase has disappeared.

THE BULLER STATUE, HELE ROAD

Naval heroes have always been plentiful in Devon, military ones less so, which may account for the adulation accorded to the pugnaciously-named General Sir Redvers Buller by Edwardian Exonians.

Buller (1839-1908) was a member of a prominent local family whose Palladian seat was at Downes, near Crediton. He joined the army aged 18 and served in China, Canada and the Gold Coast, before the Zulu War broke out in 1879. For some time small British forces were continually out-manoeuvred by the vast Zulu armies and desperate acts of heroism in tight situations were a feature of the war. A typical example occurred in March 1879 when Buller successfully led the retreat of 1,800 men from Inhlobane whilst 'hotly pursued' by 20,000 Zulus. For his personal bravery in the action he was awarded the Victoria Cross. This exploit and others fired local pride, as well it might, judging by an eye-witness description of their hero.

> Leading his men on at a swinging canter, with his reins in his teeth, a revolver in one hand and a knobkerrie he had snatched from a Zulu in the other, his hat blown off in the melée, and a large

10. Buller Statue, Hele Road.

streak of blood across his face . . . this gallant horseman seemed a demon incarnate to the flying savages . . . '.

Other campaigns followed, culminating in Buller's controversial command of the Natal Field Force during the Boer War, and the relief of Ladysmith in 1900. On his return home 50,000 admirers subscribed to commemorate the general with a larger-than-life equestrian statue commissioned from the sculptor Adrian Jones (1845-1938), himself a former vet and cavalry officer who had turned to sculpture in his thirties. The bronze statue depicts Buller in full dress uniform, and on the granite plinth are carved the words, 'He Saved Natal'. The statue is dignified, very detailed, and rather dull, as are Jones' other works, which include his masterpiece, The Quadriga, above Constitution Arch in London, completed in 1912.

BURNTHOUSE LANE ESTATE

It may seem rather far-fetched to link this modest housing estate with the garden suburb movement – but such is the case. Garden suburbs were first built by a few enlightened industrialists in the second half of the 19th century, and the idea was enthusiastically taken up by architects steeped in the socialist philosophy of William Morris and idealists like Ebenezer Howard, whose book, *Garden Cities of Tomorrow* (1902), popularised 'garden' life. The earliest suburb was built at Bedford Park in West London (begun 1876), whilst in Hampstead, Lutyens designed another (1906) which no subsequent example has matched.

In Exeter, the Burnthouse Lane Estate was the first of its kind, but here the leafy acres enjoyed in Hampstead have been condensed by rigorous municipal control. Nevertheless there are similarities – the formal overall plan, the broad roads with culs-de-sac off, the obligatory church, school, corner shops, the comfortable *Dolphin* pub and, above all, each house with its own front and back gardens separated only by hedges, not walls. The architectural style is also characteristic of the movement, unassuming brick semi-detached houses with little bracketed porches that are recognisably neo-Queen Anne. As an inspiration to the inhabitants, streets named after great literary figures were chosen for one side of the arterial road, and after trees and shrubs on the other. To them, however, it was known as 'Siberia', so far was it from their former homes in the centre of town.

11. Burnthouse Lane Estate.

THE CATHEDRAL

The cathedral is a building of superlatives. Apart from being Exeter's most distinguished building by far, it is also, except for the city walls, the largest and amongst the oldest. It stands at the centre of the city on a site first occupied by the Romans in the first century A.D. and later in the seventh century, by the monastic church of St Mary and St Peter. In 1003 the Danes burned down that church but it was rebuilt and became a cathedral in 1050 when Bishop Leofric transferred the See from Crediton. In the early 12th century, 40 years after Exeter had capitulated to the Normans, William Warelwast, a nephew of the Conqueror, was appointed bishop (1107-37) and he, as was the Norman custom, replaced the Saxon cathedral with his own mighty building.

The transept towers are all that now survive of Warelwast's church but as each is the size of a small castle keep they are ample demonstration of what must have been an awe-inspiring sight to the subjugated Saxon peasant and they have dominated the city ever since. As an architectural feature they are almost unique in England. Their only predecessor was in the Norman cathedral of Old Sarum, near Salisbury, now demolished, and their only reappearance was in the 13th century at Ottery St Mary, 12 miles to the east. Instead of Exeter's usual red sandstone they are built of grey limestone and decorated with bands of zig-zagged arcading, a favourite Norman device. The south tower has more arcading than its partner; medieval masons were never too bothered by demands for precise symmetry, but both are now terminated with 15th-century corner turrets which superseded squat spires.

One hundred and fifty years after Bishop Warelwast another bishop, Walter Bronescombe (1257-80), decided to modernise the cathedral once more in a typically unsentimental medieval way that would outrage today's conservationists. Except for the towers he demolished the entire Norman cathedral and began again at the east end. The architectural style, now known as Decorated, was then the fashion and with little variation building proceeded for the next 60 years for 300 feet to the west. Only Salisbury cathedral can match Exeter's stylistic consistency which is reinforced by the extravagant multiplication of tierceron ribs, comprising the longest unbroken span of gothic vaulting in the world, and the absence of a crossing tower junction. It is not, however, very high, only 69 feet, which is normal in English cathedrals but a great contrast to their compact French counterparts whose gothic vaults habitually topped 100 feet.

Below the vault, large clerestory windows were designed in pairs either side of the choir and nave. Their tracery does not quite flow in the sinuous shapes that are the hallmark of the developed Decorated style but as exercises in geometrical ingenuity they are unparalleled. Around their bases runs a connecting catwalk bordered by a balustrade pierced with a double row of quatrefoils. It links with the band of blind triforium arches which in turn just touch the apex of the arcade. These are profusely moulded, demonstrating anew a concern for rich surface texture which occurs again in the supporting pillars, each rippling with 16 shafts of Purbeck marble. When the cathedral was built much of the stone surface would have been painted, but colour is now concentrated on the roof bosses which have been over restored, blotting out medieval paintwork and creating an emphasis on the vault that was never originally intended.

Reading the stylistic clues to the cathedral's evolution is an intriguing game, especially in the nave where the minstrel's gallery and the variations in the carved stops to the wall shafts alone provide evidence of the building's history. The Lady Chapel starts with old-fashioned stiff leaf foliage carving which develops into more realistic plant forms, especially on the pulpitum, but by the west end has congealed into a vegetation sometimes nicknamed 'seaweed'. At that stage a new bishop, John Grandisson (1327-69), was directing the work and there seems to have been some indecision about the way in which the west end should terminate. The result is a facade on three distinct planes: the gable end, the great traceried window and, almost as an afterthought, the famous sculpture screen. Grandisson himself is buried in a small funerary chapel within the thickness of the screen which is also occupied by three rows of sculpted figures posing under their niches with disarming informality. The cross-legged attitude of some and the conversational rapport of others imbues these anonymous figures with a sense of life seldom found in medieval sculpture. They were completed by about 1375 and with them the cathedral itself.

Since then only a few changes have occurred. The cloister on the south side was rebuilt in 1377 but demolished during the Civil War. New cloisters by J. L. Pearson (1817-97) were left unfinished in 1887. The rectangular chapter house, first built in 1224, was reconstructed in 1412. It now has Perpendicular windows and an intricately-painted timber ceiling. In 1969 grey glass-fibre figures representing the Creation were installed here by the sculptor Kenneth Carter but they seem sinister and ill-at-ease in their 13th-century niches.

There are far more important furnishings in the Cathedral, in particular the bishop's throne which Pevsner described as 'the most exquisite piece of woodwork of its date in England and perhaps in Europe'. The throne is surrounded by four vast ogee arches supporting a complex series of crocketed pinnacles culminating in a skeletal spire almost reaching the high vault. It was probably built by Thomas of Winchester, where the only comparable throne can be seen, and paid for by Bishop Walter Stapledon (1308-26) who later achieved notoriety as treasurer to the disreputable Edward II and was murdered as a result by the London mob. Gilbert Scott's 19th-century choir stalls appear spindly in

12. The Cathedral.

comparison but fortunately he incorporated 49 13th-century misericords, the oldest complete set in England, and accommodated the organ, rebuilt by John Loosemore in 1665, which still dominates the view up the nave. Loosemore (1613-81) was a Devonian and this is his masterpiece. Most of the 17th-century mechanism has been replaced but amongst the great clusters of pipes was the largest of its kind in the country. Scott (1811-78) restored the cathedral in the 1870s and in doing so incurred the wrath of many who wanted the nave 'skreen' (also by Thomas of Winchester) and organ moved. Scott refused and was criticised for being 'too slight and finicking'.

Like all cathedrals, Exeter is a repository of fine sculpture in the memorials to its bishops and county families. There are too many for a detailed record here but among the best is the effigy of Bishop Bronescombe in the Lady Chapel, reputedly the work of Westminster craftsmen with original green, red and yellow paint still adhering to the black basalt figure, and the defaced (mainly in the 17th century) alabaster effigy of Bishop Edward Stafford (1395-1419) opposite. In a wall tomb on the north wall of the chapel lie the recumbent polychrome figures of Sir John Dodderidge (1555-1628), a Solicitor-General and his wife (died 1614), represented wearing a spectacular embroidered and lace dress which retains its original Jacobean colours. In the south ambulatory are a pair of rugged looking cross-legged stone knights: Sir Henry Ralegh (died 1303), and Humphrey Bohun, Earl of Hereford (killed at the Battle of Borough Bridge in 1322), and opposite a Tudor bishop, William Cotton (1598-1621) reclining on his back. The north ambulatory aisle houses Sir Robert Stapledon (died 1320), brother of the murdered bishop (whose tomb is also here), dressed in armour with his horse and page either side, and the ancient Purbeck marble effigy of Bishop Henry Marshall (1194-1206). Nearer the north transept is a ghastly emaciated gisant, or memento mori, railed off in a niche (there is another in the transept), and beyond that Bishop Valentine Carey (1621-26) recumbent but resplendent in painted alabaster within his Renaissance tomb.

The south transept contains two very elegant family groups: the soldier Sir Hugh Courtenay (died 1377) and his wife lying on a gothic tomb chest, and Sir John Gilbert and his wife in a canopy tomb but now devoid of paint. Finally, no visit to the cathedral is complete without examination of the memorial in the north aisle to the officers and men of the 9th Queen's Royal Lancers who died, heroically, during the Indian Mutiny. They are represented by two bronze mounted horsemen and palm trees by Baron Marochetti (1805-67), Prince Albert's favourite sculptor.

There are many other treasures in the cathedral, like the full-size brass memorial to Sir Peter Courtenay (died 1409), the 15th-century clock in the north transept (and an even older clock movement next to it), the early medieval stained glass in the east window and the little font dated 1692: the list is long and distinguished but it is the architecture and sculpture which are the building's greatest glory; details of these other things may be found in guidebooks to the cathedral.

THE CATHEDRAL CLOSE

Here is the highest concentration of Grade I listed buildings in Exeter, miraculously composed into a most picturesque architectural patchwork.

North of the group is St Martin's church (*see* p. 90) and, squeezed in beside it, the rumbustious Mol's Coffee House, a famous Exeter landmark whose facade could not be mistaken for anything but an Elizabethan building, even without the prominent addition of its date: 1596. It is tall, timber-framed, with jettied stories, each one lit by horizontal bands of casement windows, the first floor being the most complete. This, and the floor above, also command good views through the device of canted bays. The top floor supports a balcony, similar to the contemporary one on the Guildhall and it is assumed that originally it had a straight-sided gable which was reshaped, Dutch fashion, in the 19th century.

Writing in 1806, Jenkins explained the name 'Mol' referred to the Italian proprietor of the Coffee House, a superior establishment, 'regularly supplied with newspapers and other periodical publications and is frequented by gentlemen of the first distinction in the City'. By the 1830s Mol had gone and John Gendall, the Exeter artist, restorer and carriage panel painter, made the house his home for 30 years. On the first floor an oak panelled room is decorated with a frieze of 46 coats of arms, probably painted in Gendall's time. It is the best of the rooms but wasted because unused.

East of Mol's is a group of three, probably late 16th-century, timber-framed houses. Numbers 2 and 4 still retain their gable ends, No. 3, in the middle, was given a rectangular face lift in the 18th century, but not one of the interiors remains unscathed.

To the right again is No. 5, a symmetrical and horizontal facade in complete contrast to the earlier jumble of houses. It was brick built in 1688 according to the date of the rainwater head and it bears all the period hall-marks: windows behind the parapet, a bracketed projecting cornice, moulded architraves around sash windows (these are replacements) and stone quoins. The interiors of the two panelled front rooms also survive, one with a contemporary fireplace. When Trollope wrote *He Knew He Was Right* in 1869, he described the Close as a place 'in which a lady could live safely and decently'. Today he might think otherwise since it has become a teeming rendezvous for every tourist in the city, but through the carriage entrance to No. 5 is a peaceful little courtyard which he would still recognise. It is part of the Annuellars Hall, now the Exeter and County Club. Annuellars were chantry priests attached to the cathedral. At the Reformation the Order was suppressed, but their early 16th-century refectory hall survives, still happily used as the club's dining room although now divided horizontally. It has a barrel vault divided by moulded timber ribs and in the room below an oak screen, showing signs of being moved from elsewhere, and a Perpendicular-style stone fireplace with angel corbels still bearing traces of medieval paint.

Back in the Close, the next building is the creeper-covered regular facade of No. 6, the former subdeanery. The date on the downpipe is 1696, but parts of the Heavitree stone wall show signs of medieval openings now blocked, whilst the Tuscan porch is an 18th-century addition.

Number 7 is a very distinguished building. It began life as the residence of a cathedral canon, was remodelled in the 16th century and became the home of a parliamentary general, Sir William Waller, in the mid-17th century. In 1662, the Courtenays, Earls of Devon, acquired it as their Exeter town house, and so it remained until bought by the Devon and Exeter Institution in 1813, when it was extensively altered. The Heavitree stone gatehouse fronting the Close was Georgianised by inserting large sash windows and a front door with an elegant fanlight. (The facade has recently been spoiled by fussy, white painted cladding below the eaves.) Behind it, where there used to be a courtyard, hall and kitchen, two library rooms were built, each top lit by lanterns and now lined with bookcases on two levels, the upper half served by a gallery. The rooms have hardly changed since and the atmosphere is marvellously old fashioned – long runs of 19th century periodicals mercifully spared from the microfiche and a comfortable rag-bag of old chairs and threadbare Turkey carpets. Rather less satisfactory is the surviving low-ceilinged Tudor room at the rear whose plasterwork, including the Courtenay arms, has been overpainted with a heavy hand. It dates from about 1580 and is probably by John Abbott, one of the renowned Frithelstock family of plasterers in North Devon.

13. Cathedral Close, with Mol's Coffee House on the left.

14. No. 10, Cathedral Close.

Numbers 8 and 9 form one block, now a solicitor's office. The front is clearly medieval in origin with a Heavitree stone ground floor supporting oak brackets on which a timbered facade oversails. Two large bow windows are among the 18th-century alterations to the building, but none of this prepares one for the 15th-century hall reached through the arch and at right angles to the front. It is two storeys high and three bays long with a single hammer beam roof that is unique in Exeter. Angels bearing painted shields serve as carved terminals to the hammer beams and a blocked smoke vent can still be seen in the apex of the roof. The hall has always had legal connections and was, perhaps, an ecclesiastical court, but it has been ruthlessly partitioned by the Church Commissioners and now languishes as an office accounts department. In her book *The English Medieval House*, Margaret Wood compares the roof to that of Westminster Hall 'the finest piece of carpentry in Europe'. Surely the city and commissioners could put this hall to better use?

Adjacent to the far end of the hall is another substantial brick house dating from about 1700 and known as the Notaries House. It is still used by solicitors who so often occupy the best offices in cathedral cities.

One of the most picturesque buildings in Exeter is the Archdeacon's House at No. 10 which enjoys its own wisteria-hung courtyard. The oak door to this is carved in a fantastic cubed design with a fan top, similar to its contemporary at the Guildhall (i.e. about 1600). Above it, carved in stone, are the arms of Bishop Cotton (1598-1621). This front range probably contained the stables. Across the courtyard is the two-storey hall with three tall windows and, above the door into the screens passage, the arms of another bishop, Hugh Oldham (1504-19), founder of Manchester Grammar School and co-founder of Corpus Christi College, Cambridge. To its left is the chapel with a Perpendicular east window and, inside, a plastered 17th-century wagon roof. The gabled west range, now harshly painted in black and white, was heavily restored in the 19th century. During the early 19th century the Exeter artist, John Gendall, lived here and probably introduced the neo-classical friezes by Flaxman and Thorwaldsen and other interior features which have been considered 'suspect'.

The remaining two houses in the terrace, Nos. 11 and 12, were badly damaged in the Blitz on 24 April 1942, and have been virtually rebuilt. Inside No. 11 a medieval open timber roof and stone fireplace survive, but No. 12, a gatehouse to the former Abbot's Lodge behind it, has only the entrance arch remaining.

On the opposite side of the road, behind high walls, is No. 15, now part of the Cathedral Choir School. Its origins are medieval, but in the 18th century its size was doubled by Chancellor Furseman (died 1727), who built a brick seven-bay east front under a central pediment. One panelled room of this period survives despite the inevitable changes made by the school (especially the overwhelming fire precautions). This must be Miss Stanbury's house described by Trollope:

> . . . so close to the east end of the [Cathedral] that a carriage could not be brought quite up to her door. It was a large brick house, very old, with a door in the middle and five steps ascending to it between high iron rails. On each side of the door there were three tiers of five windows each and the house was double throughout having as many windows looking out behind into a gloomy courtyard.

The exit from the Close towards Southernhay is spanned by an elegant iron bridge, cast in 1814, which links a break in the city walls. The names of the city's enlightened mayor and receiver in that year are inscribed on its graceful neo-classical arches. To the north, standing within its own gardens, is a dull neo-Tudor house of grey stone. It was built for the Archdeacon of Cornwall by Charles Fowler in 1830.

15. Statue of John Hooker, Cathedral Green

THE CATHEDRAL GREEN

As its name implies, this is a pleasant grassy sward, but 10 feet beneath the surface are the remains of an enormous Roman bath house which once stood near the centre of the legionary fortress. It was built in about A.D. 60 from stone quarried at Rougemont and comprised three rooms, a cold room (*frigidarium*) containing a cold bath, a warm room (*tepidarium*) and a hot room (*caldarium*), each barrel vaulted in concrete and tile roofed. The height of these vaults was about forty feet and the entire complex covered an area comparable to the cathedral. Seventy thousand gallons of water were brought daily from natural springs to the north east of the fortress and heat supplied by two external furnace houses for both hot water and the underfloor hot air central heating system.

In about A.D. 75 the Legion moved its headquarters to Caerleon in South Wales, and Exeter became a civilian town, causing the bath house to be converted into an administrative centre. During the fifth century when the Romans retreated from Britain the bath house would have fallen into disrepair and, no doubt, was robbed of its stone so that by the 11th century a church, St Mary Major, was built on the site and rebuilt in 1865. The Roman ruins were forgotten. Pevsner described the latter church as 'major only as a disaster to the effect of the Close as a whole' (the architect was Edward Ashworth), so no one lamented its demolition in 1971, but they were happily surprised to find the bath house beneath it.

Excavations between 1971 and 1976 discovered not only the plan of the building, but fragments of mosaics, the earliest yet found in Britain, and evidence of other entertainments like cockfighting and gambling that legionaries could enjoy here. It was, in fact, a complete sports centre, the Roman equivalent of the Plaza today (*see* p. 67), and the largest of its kind known in Britain. After excavation, the site was carefully infilled, but controversial plans have been suggested for reviving it once again and turning it into a permanent exhibition.

Two other monuments enhance the Green. The most prominent is the white stone seated statue of John Hooker, the 17th-century historian of Exeter, by Alfred Drury, R.A. (1856-

1944). Drury trained in Paris under the French sculptor Jules Dalou. His best-known work is the bronze statue of another Devonian, Sir Joshua Reynolds, which stands in the courtyard of the Royal Academy.

Due west of the cathedral, beyond the cross that marks the site of St Mary Major, is a granite cross designed by Sir Edwin Lutyens (1869-1944) in memory of the men who died during the First World War. Lutyens wrote, 'it is very simple and a monolith and its subtlety in line means labour, care and thought. It is out of one stone, the biggest I could get . . . It should endure for ever'.

THE CATHEDRAL YARD

The buildings follow the line of the 13th-century north wall of the Cathedral Close. Starting at the east end is the *Royal Clarence Hotel*, more significant for its historical associations than its architecture. (It was named after the Duchess of Clarence, an early visitor, whose husband became William IV in 1827; other guests have been Lord Nelson and the future Czar Nicholas I.) It was built as the city's Assembly Rooms by William Mackworth Praed in 1768, but converted into an hotel in 1770 by a Frenchman, Peter Berlon, who was the first to use the word 'hotel' in Britain. (Robert Adam drew plans for an Assembly Room in Exeter, but these were never carried out and the architect of the present building is unknown.) In the early 19th century it was remodelled in the 'Egyptian style' and has since been altered again so that now, behind the stucco facade, the only faintly discernible style is Edwardian.

The hotel has swallowed up its neighbours. 'Orchards' to the north was formerly the premises of the Exeter Bank; on the other side is a pair of gabled 17th-century houses, one known as the Well House where, six feet down in the cellar, a Roman well and bath have been excavated.

All this is predictable in Exeter; No. 18 is anything but. It was built at the end of the 19th century and bears the period hallmarks of large plate-glass windows and ponderous ornament – especially a profusion of egg-and-dart mouldings and an elaborate cornice. There is a theory that it was built by a curio collector with a fancy for the French Renaissance, hence perhaps the Mansard roof, and it was certainly a curious person who dreamt up the interior. A staircase rises through the centre of the building. The first flight is 18th century in style surrounded at first floor level by a gallery. Off this are a number of rooms each entered through dark mahogany doors, framed by Corinthian pilasters, but with the disconcerting addition of mirrored panels. The effect is wierdly surreal. A large room (now divided into two) overlooking the cathedral is equally strange. Beneath a gilded cornice are walls panelled with large mirrors festooned with glass drops and bordered by wallpaper in the Pompeian style. At each end are highly polished black fireplaces supported by stone lions. At present these exotic rooms are used as solicitors' offices, which seems rather a waste.

Continuing south, beyond a dull block of Georgian pastiche, is another change of style, High Victorian gothic built in 1883 for the ecclesiastical outfitters and church furnishers, Messrs. Wippells. Although the firm has recently moved from this site, it continues to supply stained glass and metalwork for churches all over the world from its manufacturing base in Okehampton Street.

At the end of the terrace is Tinley's Café, which is worth visiting on two counts. Firstly, behind the 19th-century facade are the remnants of the Close wall, built to provide security for the clergy after the murder of Walter Lechlade, the first precentor of the cathedral in 1275. Secondly, the cafe itself is an anachronism having somehow escaped change since the 1930s, so it is exactly how a Cathedral Close teashop should be, old-fashioned, comfortable and rather eccentric.

16. Little Stile, Cathedral Yard.

17. City bank, Cathedral Yard.

To the left of Tinley's is the site of the old Broadgate, one of seven entrances to the Close demolished in 1825, and to the left of that is Exeter's finest bank building, the City Bank, designed by John Gibson (1817-92) in 1875. Gibson was an architect who specialised in Renaissance style bank buildings with a nationwide practice. This classical facade, dignified, symmetrical and with a most imposing entrance, was guaranteed to reassure the customers.

Opposite the bank is Little Stile, a terrace of three gabled houses. These date from the mid-17th century and were first occupied by craftsmen working on the cathedral. Each has a cellar lined with Heavitree stone and a timber framed construction above. Top floor five light oriel windows appear original, but elsewhere major changes have occurred and as always the interiors have suffered the most, although behind the Victorian facade of No. 4 is a quaint Dickensian suite of offices.

CATHERINE STREET AND ST MARTIN'S LANE

Numbers 1 and 2 Catherine Street are small lop-sided gabled shops that fill this corner of the Cathedral Close with just the right picturesque disorder. They date from the 15th century and may well be the houses described in a contemporary document as north of St Martin's church whose stonework John Whytten, a mason, agreed to build on 14 September 1404 for £6 6s. 8d. The contract specified two gables at each end, two chimneys in the upper rooms, two latrines, two doors and four windows.

The cellars and rear wall are indeed built of Heavitree stone, each has a garderobe on the first floor (blocked off in No. 1 and converted into a cupboard in No. 2) and there are fireplaces in No. 2. During the 16th century the joists in No. 1 were painted with black and yellow chevron designs, traces of which can still be seen on the first floor. More recently the windows have been replaced and the cut slate hanging reproduced but the facades nevertheless remain convincing.

The houses were probably built to accommodate priests serving the cathedral but they were converted into shops during the 17th century. To their south is St Martin's Lane, still medieval in width, where posts commemorate the removal of St Martin's Gate in 1819, one of five gates bordering the Cathedral Close. Here too is the *Ship Inn*, apparently frequented by Sir Francis Drake in the late 16th century. Architecturally it now seems a mainly 20th-century restoration save a solid stone fireplace in the bar, the only feature Drake would recognise in a horrible kitsch interior.

At the other end of Catherine Street are the bombed remains of medieval almshouses, consolidated as a memorial to the Blitz (*see* p. 85).

CLAREMONT GROVE

Over the last 150 years St Leonards has developed into the most sought after of Exeter's suburban parishes, but in the 1820s it was still part of an agricultural estate attached to the Baring family home, Mount Radford. Changes began during the early 19th century when the city's population doubled to 40,000 and the banker, Sir Thomas Baring, succumbed to the temptation by selling his home to building speculators for new housing. The successful purchaser was the Hooper family (*see* p. 2) who demolished Mount Radford and converted its drive into St Leonard's, Road bounded by houses designed for 'clergymen, physicians, colonels, plain one thousand a year folk, given to talk about quarter sessions and the new road bill . . .'. Next, Wonford Road was built to bisect St Leonards and more houses added, sometimes in terraces, sometimes surrounded by a leafy garden and sometimes laid out in a formal group like a crescent or square, but always stuccoed and often enhanced with verandahs and fanciful ironwork.

There were two popular architectural styles: gothic, as in Nos. 36 to 40 Wonford Road,

18. Catherine Street and St Martin's Lane.

19. No. 2, Claremont Grove.

and classical, like the semi-detached villas in The Quadrant. Claremont Grove, which is a miniature but superior housing estate, one of several built in Exeter during the early 19th century, has more variety. Number 1 is gingerbread, early Victorian with broad decorative barge boards to the gables and gothic windows. Number 2 has a castellated parapet and a cluster columned gothic porch, whilst No. 3 is gaunt Tudor with flattened arches over the windows, beneath drip moulds. The Grove is approached by a private drive guarded at the gate by a small lodge with a ground plan once described as 'two jointed octagons'. Surrounding the houses are the remnants of old cob garden walls and trees, part of the original pleasure grounds. Despite bomb damage in 1942, the inevitable divisions into flats and insensitive repairs (usually to windows where glazing bar patterns are ignored), the old stately pace of life once enjoyed by Exeter's wealthy professional classes can still be savoured here.

CLEVE HOUSE, CANTERBURY ROAD

This is yet another fine house recently engulfed by suburbia leaving no option but conversion to institutional use, in this case the regional centre for Guide Dogs for the Blind which moved here in the 1950s. Alterations have included two new administration blocks at the rear and a lavish redecoration scheme in 1988 that have swamped the period details not least in gallons of white gloss paint. The result is an antiseptic shell that contradicts the 1947 Grade II* listing which describes the house as 'well modernised'.

The present L-shaped house was built by the Northmore family in Charles II's reign and remodelled in the 18th century, which accounts for the Venetian window above a Tuscan porch. These alterations probably date from the 1770s as the house was advertised to let in 1778 and referred to as 'modern built' in 'a situation exceeded by none'. It comprised a hall, three parlours, a dining room and 'good lodging rooms' for the accommodation 'of a large genteel family'.

Today, the only 17th-century features are the camouflaged finials of a staircase and the room to the left of the entrance hall. This retains its panelled dado and a boldly modelled plaster ceiling divided by borders of laurel leaves. The floral central oval is inhabited by a lion, eagle, horse and birds and at either end a duck (or goose) with a crown around its neck. Elsewhere, the hall is attractively paved in black and white, a few rooms still have sections of moulded panelling and there is a nice 19th-century staircase with turned balusters but the restoration has been so thorough that the overall effect is very muted.

COLLETON CRESCENT

The Crescent is the only one of Matthew Nosworthy's Exeter housing schemes (*see* p. 9) completed as planned and surviving intact. It was built high above the river in the 1800s on the same grand scale as the earlier Barnfield Crescent and with the same Coade stone voussoirs as contemporary Southernhay. It is a glorious position appreciated and painted by J. M. W. Turner.

At each end of the Crescent are three-storey houses flanked by pilasters. Adjoining them are four-storey houses with Nosworthy's double-arched windows on the ground floor and string courses between each floor. The centre group of five houses is stepped forward and is a little higher than the rest, a rather clumsy device. Two of them are distinguished by exceptionally fine verandas enclosed in a delicate iron network. The Flemish bond brickwork was originally tuck pointed, using a white coloured chalk-lime putty, and the contrast between this precise technique and later repointing with ordinary mortar is noticeable.

The Crescent is named after the Colleton merchant family of Exeter. John Colleton introduced a species of magnolia to this country from Carolina in 1737 and it was a Louisa Colleton who laid the foundation stone of the Crescent on 3 September 1802. Most of the houses are now converted to office use but some original staircases, pine panelling and plasterwork survive.

At the west end of the Crescent is Riverside Court, a crudely classical styled block of flats built in 1973, designed by David Saxon of Bristol. The best that can be said of it is that the railings are good. The Court itself is hopelessly muddled in plan, proportions and detail. It replaces a demolished early 19th-century house. Opposite is Colleton House, a large stuccoed Greek Revival house. A pediment spans the three bays and a central Ionic porch.

CONGREGATIONAL CHURCH, FORE STREET, HEAVITREE

Approached from the east the church conjures up a Perpendicular gothic nightmare as four storeys of mullioned windows soar between ranks of red brick buttresses topped by an

20. Cleve House, Canterbury Road.

21. Colleton Crescent.

unusual number of gables and an octagonal spirelet. It is splendid provincial stuff, the work of Frederick J. Commin, an architect whose name appears on the foundation stone and better known for his baroque style Methodist church in Sidwell Street (*see* p. 109). Move inside, however, and the building makes more sense for it assumes a range of uses besides the church itself, with a basement lecture hall, vestries and, once, 10 classrooms.

The church interior is spacious and remarkably unspoiled. Deal pews, with brass umbrella stands intact, are aligned on a slightly raked floor. The deal wainscot, pale buff brick walls, charming floral designed stained-glass windows, reminiscent of front parlours, and an elaborate pine tie-beam roof are also Edwardian survivors. The pulpit dominates the west end and a gallery the east. The building had a lucky escape in 1942 when a bomb destroyed next door houses but blew out only the east window.

22. Congregational church, Fore Street, Heavitree.

COUNTY HALL, BELLAIR AND COAVER, TOPSHAM ROAD

The county is lucky to have these headquarters, which were built in neo-Georgian style and traditional materials between 1958 and 1964, a time when most architects were busily designing blocks of glass and steel. (Only Bristol and Winchester have comparable public buildings of the period.) The architect was Donald McMorran (died 1965) who had worked as an assistant to Vincent Harris, the university architect, and is best known in London for his Old Bailey extension and Wood Street Police Station, both in the same neo-Georgian style with characteristic segmental-headed windows.

County Hall is planned around a courtyard and constructed to a very high standard using granite, brick and slate. Nowhere does it rise above four storeys, apart from the belltower, itself reduced in height by 30 feet to save expense. The interiors are equally impressive, particularly the spacious council chamber and committee rooms panelled in native Devon hardwoods.

23. County Hall and Bellair, Topsham Road.

24. Cowick Barton, Cowick Lane.

The whole complex stands in spacious grounds formerly attached to Bellair, the brick Queen Anne villa to the west. This was built by John Vowler, an Exeter grocer and last inhabited by Dame Georgiana Buller, who died in 1953. Surviving inside is some panelling, the original staircase and some fruity plasterwork (probably by the Abbott family), but 18th-century elegance has been largely smothered by the garish conversion of the house into a 'lounge and rest room' for council members. A heavy municipal hand has also taken its toll of the garden where the rows of red tulips are more suited to a traffic island than here. West of Bellair is a second villa, Coaver, built in the early 19th century for the Mitford family of bankers. It has suffered even more from a recent conversion – into a staff social centre. The ground floor has been gutted and refurnished to resemble any other dralon-draped saloon bar.

COWICK BARTON, COWICK LANE

The surprising thing about this classic Tudor farmhouse is its situation, off a busy suburban road in the middle of an unremarkable housing estate. It is not the obvious place to find a three-storey E-plan pub, but that is what it became in 1963 after a chequered history.

The assumption is that it began life as the farm attached to Cowick Priory; this had been dissolved before 1539 but after the Dissolution its land was given to Lord Russell, Lord Lieutenant of Devon. It seems likely he built the present house which would account for a stained-glass panel formerly in a window depicting the arms of Edward VI as Prince of Wales. (The panel is now in the Victoria and Albert Museum, which should be asked to replace it with a copy.) For a while the house was the home of the White-Abbott family, including John White-Abbott (1763-1851) the water colourist and his grandson, who restored it.

The house is built of Heavitree stone, rendered and painted pale green at the time of writing, with the exception of the centre wing. Nearly all the stone mullioned windows survive. Entrance, as always, is through the porch at the centre of the E, but the cross-passage within has gone, creating one long room. On one side was the kitchen, on the other the hall, each with a cavernous fireplace, one now filled with tiles in the fashionable Japanese style of the 1890s, above which is the date 1657 and the arms of the Baron family. In the north wing is another fireplace with a vast overmantle depicting several little figures and an obscure reference to St Paul's epistle to the Philippians. It is a pity that it is now painted in garish colours, which are both crude and unhistorical.

North of the river the pub would be a honeypot for tourists, but lost in St Thomas's the heritage trails and guidebooks make no mention of it. It functions as a result like any other unpretentious 'local'.

THE CUSTOMS HOUSE, THE QUAY

The earliest settlement of Exeter was for geographic reasons: at a point marking the tidal limit of river navigation for ships, a hardstone quay and a valley route through the rocky cliffs above. Today the site is occupied by the Customs House, built as such in 1681 and still used for the purpose with responsibility for all ports from Teignmouth to Lyme Regis. The architect was Richard Allen about whom nothing seems known, but his building is typical of its date: a brick-built symmetrical facade, large windows, hipped gables, and a pediment. It is the earliest surviving brick building in Exeter; others dating back to the 1650s in Magdalen Street were demolished in 1977.

During 300 years changes have occurred. A two-bay extension on one side is the most obvious; sash windows have replaced the leaded originals, some of which remain at the rear, and the open colonnaded ground floor has been filled in.

In 1698 Celia Fiennes, an energetic traveller and diary writer, visited Exeter and described the Customs House with its 'open space below with rows of pillars, which they lay in goods just as they are loaded off the ships in case of wet . . .'. She omits to mention the great stove installed at this level and used for burning contraband goods, but she did 'ascend up the handsome pair of stairs into a large room full of desks and little partitions for the writers and accountants. It was full of books and piles of papers'. The staircase is still there with hefty turned balusters and a broad handrail. Panelling and pigeon holes also survive, but most stunning of all upstairs are three baroque plaster ceilings by John Abbott (1639-1727).

25. Customs House, The Quay.

Abbott came from a family of plasterers in Frithelstock, North Devon, who compiled a pattern book illustrating their work over a period of about 150 years. It includes the Customs House ceilings for which he was paid £35. The one over the staircase, with its broad floral circle, only hints at the excesses of the other two. In the Surveyors's Room the octagonal centre is surrounded by lavish ribbon swags and outer panels of various shapes. The flowers and ribbons are completely naturalistic and overflow in a high relief made possible by the use of wooden pegs and a lead wire framework. Next door the Longroom ceiling is dominated by an oval of intertwined oak branches inhabited by grotesque masks and eels which twist perilously from the foliage. In a county famous for its decorated plasterwork, the Customs House ceilings are among the finest.

THE DEANERY, PALACE GATE

Due to a history of changing uses and frequent modernisation by progressive deans, this is a complicated building. The Romans built a bath-house here, now covered by the garden,

26. The Deanery, Palace Gate.

27. Digby Hospital, Woodwater Lane.

and the Augustinians a nunnery before the deanery was founded in the 13th century on the appointment of Serlo as Exeter's first dean in 1225.

The earliest part of the building is now the north wing. Here, above the oak beams in what is presently a dining room, is a 15th-century chapel, barrel vaulted with a three-light Perpendicular window. During the 18th century it was converted into a bedroom and the panelling is probably contemporary, but it was restored as a chapel in the 19th century and extended by the addition of a north aisle.

The more impressive south range 'of uneven width' is dominated by the 15th-century great hall, four bays long, galleried at the east end and covered by an oak arch-braced roof designed in the distinctive Exeter manner (*see* the Guildhall, p. 43). On the south wall are four windows, once rectangular, but altered in the 1760s to contain William Peckitt's painted armorial glass. Peckitt (1731-95) was a self-taught Yorkshireman and the foremost stained glass artist of his day. He practised mainly in the north, but his most important work was the west window in Exeter Cathedral. Here he has signed one of the windows which is dated 1768. On the wall opposite a vast rectangular stone traceried fireplace with heraldic shields on the mantelpiece is typical of its period, the 1490s. It was brought here from the demolished Precentor's House and resembles another, also demolished, in the Vicar's Choral (*see* page 121).

A panel in the hall records the visit to the deanery by William III in 1688, *en route* from Torbay to London. Forty years earlier, during the Commonwealth, the deanery had been converted into tenements and had reached a state 'not only ruinous, but filthy and loathesome'. It was repaired at the Restoration and again in 1741 under the direction of the energetic Dean Clarke (*see* page 80) and a second panel records another royal visitor, George III, in 1789.

Panelling in the undercroft to the hall and a plaster frieze depicting putti garlanding the head of a lady, suggest an early 17th-century date, whilst the 18th century is represented in the staircase tower with its own gothick style panelling. This would be the contribution of Dean Buller who improved the house, 'in such a manner as to render it not unworthy of the habitation of Princes', and so it has remained.

DIGBY HOSPITAL, WOODWATER LANE

This is the youngest of Exeter's three sprawling mental hospitals built by the Victorians on the outskirts of the city. The architect was Robert Stark Wilkinson (1844-1936), an Exonian with a London office, who won the commission in competition with 40 others, having produced the drawings during a single weekend in 1884. Ten years previously he had designed premises for the Doulton Ceramic Company in London and now at the Digby he made full use of Doulton's terracotta tiles in broad courses along the red brick walls, around the windows and in crisp details.

The architectural style can be vaguely described as Flemish Renaissance, particularly evident in the small spires and shaped gables. The plan was old-fashioned – a long single block design that had been popularised by the enormous Netley Military Hospital, Hampshire, in the 1860s, but criticised by Florence Nightingale who advocated separate pavilions. On the other hand her arguments for sunshine and fresh air were acknowledged here by the rows of large sash windows. Day rooms filled the ground floor and dormitories above; male patients in the east wing, females in the west. Until the 1930s the wards were heated by open fires; walls were painted brown and cream, but brightened up with framed posters and, incongruously, glass cases containing stuffed birds.

Surrounding the hospital were acres of land once successfully cultivated by the patients, but gradually new buildings have begun to fill the space and policy on mental health care has changed. In 1985 the Victorian hospital building was closed and re-development plans proposed. At the time of writing, the outcome of these proposals remains to be seen.

DIX'S FIELD

There is no more poignant reminder of what Exeter lost in the Blitz than to compare photographs of Dix's Field, taken in about 1924 for Richardson and Gill's book *Regional Architecture in the South West*, with the present pathetic remnant. Even after the war the facades and some ironwork remained of 23 listed houses in three blocks on both sides of the street. There are now four, and all heavily over-restored. The rest have been demolished for the banal Civic Centre (with its own nuclear bunker), 1969, by the city architect, Vinton Hall; a dreary Congregational church house, where the Rev. Sabine Gould's birthplace once stood and, in 1988, a dull commercial development including pastiche Georgian facades hiding strip-lighted open-plan offices.

The street was named after Mr. William Dix and originally designed in 1808 by Matthew Nosworthy (*see* p. 9). It comprised two opposing Georgian blocks with a total of 24 houses separated by a green described as 'a classic piece of architectural grouping'. Other notable residents were Sir Henry Carew, Bt., Henry Blackhall three times mayor of Exeter, Joseph Palmer, Dean of Cashel, and Nosworthy himself.

EGYPTIAN HOUSE, HOLLOWAY STREET

Egyptian influence on English architecture was at its height during the Napoleonic Wars when military expeditions to the Nile had cultural as well as strategic results. Two of the finest buildings in Britain in this esoteric style were built in the west country: P. F. Robinson's Egyptian House in Penzance, *c.* 1830 (he was also architect of the Egyptian Hall in Piccadilly), and John Foulston's Public Library in Stonehouse of 1823.

Exeter's only domestic contribution is rather less distinguished. It begins well enough with the characteristic converging lines of walls, windows and door, but fades away into a conventional classical pediment and oculus. More recently the house has been subject to every possible indignity. Derelict in the 1970s, it was converted into flats in 1981 so that today one small fireplace and an unremarkable ceiling rose is all that survives of the original interior. Worse still, any charms of living there have been blighted by the constant flow of traffic past its doorstep.

EXETER SCHOOL, VICTORIA PARK ROAD

Amongst the eminent practitioners of High Victorian architecture only William Butterfield (1814-1900) made a real impression on rural Devon, especially its churches – at Alfington, Babbacombe, Ottery St Mary, Plymouth and Yealmpton, whilst in Exeter the school was his major work. This had been founded in 1863 with premises off the High Street (now Princesshay), from which it moved in 1880 to its present spacious 25-acre site. At the same time it was intended to upgrade 'what was essentially a school for tradesmen and the better class of working men' into a higher class establishment which Butterfield was ideally suited to design. He was then nearing the end of a distinguished career, but had yet to complete two of his finest buildings: All Saints, Babbacombe and the celebrated Keble College, Oxford, whose chapel was paid for by William Gibbs (*see* p. 97).

The school would be his 'most complete boarding school scheme' (it cost £16,750; the land had been bought for £7,600). It comprises a long north wing lit by rows of lancet windows with classrooms on the ground floor, studies above, dormitories on the second floor and servants' rooms in the attic. The overall impression is imposing but rather forbidding,

28. Dix's Field.

29. Egyptian House, Holloway Street.

and the west wing which housed the kitchens and dining hall is more successful, being articulated by a series of six buttresses and terminating in a vestigial transept. Where the two wings meet a monumental six-storey tower, intended for staff rooms, fills the angle.

30. Exeter School, Victoria Park Road.

A gargoyle cornice projects at its fifth-floor level, the same height that Butterfield planned to build the roof ridge of a great schoolroom to the east – but that was never built and 100 years later raw toothing for the addition remains untouched.

Butterfield was a high-church architect, both personally and professionally, and the exuberant gothic of his buildings reflects this, particularly the emphasis on surface decoration which is the essence of his High Victorian style. Unlike Regency and early Victorian architects he revelled in using undisguised brickwork – contrasting colours to create mural patterns. Here, red Culm Davy bricks are interspersed with diamond patterns of blue-black bricks and horizontal courses of pale stone. It is vintage Butterfield architecture which at Keble coined the much-quoted description 'streaky bacon style'.

In 1885 Exeter had a chapel added, described by those who use it as 'a modest and efficient building' and with it Butterfield's work was complete. Since then, as with most institutions of this kind, a haphazard series of additions have been built, often at the expense of planning and design which have been forfeited in the quest for economy and utility.

At first there were conscientious efforts to emulate Butterfield's work, like the 1930s Andrews Library block to the north of the original north wing. It is a worthy, if dull, attempt. Thirty years later no attempt was made to harmonise with the Victorian work, resulting in the dreary brick blocks of the art room and adjoining form rooms which link up to the rear of the Paul Building Assembly Hall (1965). The arrogant indifference of this grey brick block to its red brick neighbour and Butterfield's original plans for an assembly hall east of the tower is startling, even for a 1960s building. Fortunately, the recent post-modernist trends have produced a far more imaginative classroom block in 1985 (the Richard Daw Building) by the Exeter architects Redfern, Gilpin and Riley. Proper respect was paid to Butterfield's work by using red brick patterned with a darker diaper and matching the curious basket-like iron finial on Butterfield's tower with another like it. Only the half-timbered gables seem out of place. The same architects also designed the new gates nearby which attempt, rather self-consciously, to provide a formal entrance to what is, in fact, the school's back door.

EYE HOSPITAL, MAGDALEN STREET

There has been an Eye Hospital in Exeter since 1808, but the present building dates from 1899. A foundation stone at the base records the facts about its construction and another stone in the pediment bears the date of its completion – 1901. From the front the plan is L-shaped, with a brass bound front door flanked by brick turrets that soar through three

31. Eye Hospital, Magdalen Street.

storeys and culminate in leafy cornices either side of an elongated broken pediment. The style is a hybrid baroque, so it is no surprise to learn that the architect was Sir Alfred Brumwell Thomas (1868-1948), one of the most flamboyant and successful practitioners of this Edwardian speciality. Public buildings were his forté, particularly town halls (e.g., Belfast, Woolwich and Stockport), schools and hospitals; at Exeter one need look no further than the looping front wall, negotiating corners with a bold disregard for geometry, to appreciate his bravura.

The interior has, of course, been modernised, although the entrance hall, fitted out with a marble fireplace taken from a house formerly on this site, brass door hinges and terrazzo floor, still has period flavour. The only other room that retains it is, surprisingly, the operating theatre. Here the original terrazzo floor, green tiles and oak window frames survive and there is even a fireplace in one corner (now blocked up). The hospital was designed with four wards, ample consulting rooms and its own garden, at a total cost of £25,000. It seems a modest sum for such an imposing building. In a few years' time it will be redundant, when a new and sympathetic use should be found.

FORE STREET

This is probably the oldest of all Exeter's streets because of its proximity to the original bridging point over the river, but recently its importance has declined owing to the steep gradient which has deterred new development. The majority of buildings date from the 18th and 19th centuries and they are unpretentious, but among them are the medieval Tuckers' Hall (*see* p. 113) and two exceptional buildings on the west side, numbers 143 and 144. Until bombs destroyed it, Fowler's Lower Market on the site of St George's Hall was another, but nothing of that now stands.

Number 143 Fore Street is a superior early 18th-century town house built for Sir Thomas Bury, a city merchant. During the second half of the century it was occupied by Sir John Duntze, a wool merchant and partner in the Exeter Bank and in the 19th century Thomas Latimer printed the *Western Times* here. In 1905 the new residents, Wheatons, the publishers, moved the original hooded front door to the back and added the present shop front and glazed first floor, thereby camouflaging the original four-storey house. This is five bays wide with the centre projecting slightly. Interest is provided by the use of stone in the

32. No. 143, Fore Street.

quoins, cornice and keystones, and alternating the red stretcher bricks with dark burnt headers. Unfortunately, except for a staircase with twisted balusters, nothing notable survives within.

The front of 144 is an architectural sport, with decorated timber panels and frieze above a shop front divided by a diamond-patterned column. It dates from the early 19th century, but hides a 17th-century interior, recently gutted by fire and commercial exigencies, but still preserving a remarkable decorated plaster ceiling on the first floor. The main panel features the head of a large salmon surrounded by lobsters and hounds among vine scrolls. Other panels depict hawks and a snake. It is naive but vigorous work and is presumably intended to portray the 17th-century equivalent of field sports.

FRANKLYN HOUSE, FRANKLYN DRIVE

One of many large houses once standing in its own grounds, now engulfed by suburbia and forsaken by the banking family that built it. Institutional use has proved the only alternative, in this case the Health Authority.

The house dates from the mid-18th century (the date 1757 appears on rainwater heads), but it is untouched by Palladianism – which had reached Bath in the 1730s. Instead it is a chaste brick building with broad eaves and dormers and a front door set off by a baroque flourish. Surprisingly the entrance front seems little changed from the time the Victorians substituted plate glass windows for the original heavy glazing bars and small panes. The fire escape has, thankfully, been placed to one side.

The interior is now camouflaged in layers of pastel shaded paint, but here and there are some original features – panelling, described in the 1947 listing as having 'heavy turned balusters and carved vases and flowers to newel caps' (the latter now gone), a boxed-in staircase, and best of all, an exuberantly moulded plaster ceiling in the earlier west-country tradition.

FRIAR'S WALK

The road is named after the Franciscan Priory which occupied this site from 1303 to the dissolution of the monasteries, with the present five pairs of semi-detached houses being far removed from medieval monasticism. They are urbane stuccoed neo-classical villas built in 1833 by John Mitchell, similar in style to some of John Foulston's work in Plymouth where he often built broad bracketed eaves and pilasters decorated with incised honeysuckle flourishes. Buildings with such precise proportions and detail suffer more than most from unsympathetic alterations, which have already marked this Exeter group. Further changes should be kept to a minimum, not an impossibility with listed buildings.

At the north end of the road, the plain pedimented building is a former Quaker Meeting House (1868) with a spacious octagonal room inside, partly surrounded by a columned gallery. It has been absorbed by the Salvation Army whose own brick citadel with crow-stepped gables (1890, a Mr. Dunford was the architect) stands next door. Both have suffered from an expensive plague of aluminium replacement windows.

GEORGE'S MEETING, SOUTH STREET

The east side of South Street boasts four places of worship and of these George's Meeting is the oldest and architecturally the most distinguished. It was founded as a Presbyterian chapel in 1760, the date of George III's accession, hence its name, and built on a scale unsurpassed by any other chapel in the south west.

An imposing street front bears the hallmark of non-conformist severity but tempered with elegant 18th-century flourishes. The pedimented porch is supported on a pair of stone

33. Franklyn House, Franklyn Drive.

34. Friar's Walk.

Tuscan columns and the facade itself is built of brick, punctuated by large, well-proportioned windows, ornamented only by a keystone and two brackets each. The centre bay, however, projects slightly to provide the necessary accent and this emphasis is continued in the curve of the shaped parapet. Below it a bold cornice meets the rendered quoins either side, thereby framing the entrance.

35. George's Meeting, South Street.

Pondering on the design of churches in 1711, Sir Christopher Wren recommended 'auditories', in which the congregation could 'hear distinctly, and see the Preacher'; George's Meeting fulfils those demands admirably. The interior is a plain rectangle beneath a flat plaster ceiling. Oak panelled galleries, supported on Ionic columns, extend around three sides, leaving, as the focus of attention opposite the entrance, a canopied pulpit and reading desk. This is decorated with florid carving and was brought here from St James's, the previous chapel built in 1687 (and demolished in 1960). Beyond the east end a lecture hall was added in the late 19th century (now a restaurant), and in the north-east angle with the chapel is a tiny graveyard.

George's Meeting sustained a congregation until the last war when membership steadily declined until even the building faced dereliction. In 1987 it was sold and converted into a shopping centre, but its Grade I listing has been proof against drastic change and, happily, most of the fittings survive (self-consciously) beneath coats of white paint.

THE GUILDHALL, HIGH STREET

A Guildhall has stood on this site since the 14th century, and possibly much earlier, for there is record of an Exeter Guildhall dating from the 12th century, but what one now sees is a hotchpotch of a building dating from the 15th to the 19th centuries, with the portico, as the most prominent feature, dated 1594. Renovation in 1970 revealed some blocks re-used from an older building with carving on their rear faces.

After the cathedral, this portico is Exeter's best known architectural landmark, an Elizabethan *tour de force* aptly described as 'barbarous' (Summerson) and 'picturesque'

(Pevsner), rather than elegant. It is an exact contemporary of the prodigy houses, Montacute and Hardwick, all three classically inspired but adapted and decorated in a most inventive and unrestrained manner. The portico is built out into the highway, supported on hefty granite columns. From their capitals, mighty Beer stone corbels spring steadily outwards to support eight pairs of fluted columns, which flank large expanses of mullioned and transomed windows. Strap-work decoration, a Flemish device, is much in evidence, especially on the arch soffits. During one of the many repair programmes on the portico (in 1899 when steel girders were inserted to pin it back), it was noticed that 'until about 40 years ago the front was periodically cleaned down and coloured cream colour, the frieze, flutes to columns and sinkings being picked out in red, the columns being gilded, as traces of gold were visible . . .' rather like an Elizabethan painted church memorial. Blue paint traces have since been found on the upper frieze.

36. The Guildhall, High Street.

Pass under the portico, where the City's stocks once stood, through the carved oak door, dated 1593 and made by Nicholas Baggett, and you enter the sombre Council Chamber which, despite an air of antiquity, owes as much to Victorian restorations as it does to the Middle Ages. The roof is the exception. It is arch braced in construction, but above the apex of the trusses is a small barrel vault, and between the main trusses are intermediate ones with projecting bosses. The combination of these peculiarities is found in only three other Exeter buildings and in the hall at Cadhay Manor near Ottery. The main trusses rest on grotesque carved animal corbels, uncertainly identified as bears with ragged staffs, emblem of Warwick the Kingmaker who was alive at the time the roof was built in 1468.

From the centre of the roof hangs a great brass chandelier, made by Thomas Pyke of Bridgwater and brought here in 1789, but almost everything else one sees, save the pictures, is Victorian. Even the panelling, which is of Tudor origin, was heavily restored in 1887. The gallery, the vivid stained glass, the oak furniture, the stone flags on the floor, all date from 1863; so it is appropriate that above the fireplace the bust of Queen Victoria by H. H. Armstead should preside over this beguiling example of Victorian reconstruction.

Beneath the chamber is a cellar, part of the early 14th-century building, and at one time a prison known as the 'pytt of the Guyldhall'. Another prison, for women, was first built to the rear of the chamber in the 16th century and used until 1887. The room above it was added in 1858 to house the exceptional collection of City records, but later used as a jury room with panelling brought from St Katherine's Priory (*see* p. 87). Above the portico is a room used as the mayor's parlour, but once the Guildhall chapel. It was refitted in 1900 by Dart and Francis of Crediton and repaired in 1986 when, incredibly, the plaster ceiling dating from about 1800 was destroyed and a replica substituted. This should never have happened, particularly as it is now technically possible to repair old plaster.

HARLEQUIN CENTRE, PAUL STREET

'The fashionable heart of Exeter now beats a little faster . . . a new exciting shopping experience . . . the setting is elegant, the atmosphere relaxed and sophisticated' enthuses the publicity for this vulgar shopping centre which towers over Paul Street, now resembling a brick canyon sunk between two vast car parks with the Harlequin Centre cantilevered over one to contain a complex of 32 shops.

The architectural style is mongrel Hollywood classicism and old fashioned 'art deco' touched up with red and blue paint. Among the gift shops every surface gleams seductively – mirrored and glazed ceilings, brass and glass walls, polished terazzo floors. The source for

37. Harlequin Centre, Paul Street.

all this appears to be the 1960s American shopping mall, endorsed by such details as the plastic pot plants and mindless muzak. The architects were Bruges Tozer of Bristol and the cost, in 1987, £6 million.

THE HIGH STREET

This is Exeter's most important street and one of four laid out by the Romans when they first quartered the city. Today the earliest surviving buildings are 16th century, hardy survivors of sieges, modernisation, road widening and the Blitz, which have all helped shape the street into what is now a microcosm of post-medieval architectural history.

Among these tenacious relics are Nos. 225-6 (C.& A.), originally a pair of timber-framed houses, probably built in 1576 by Thomas Prestwood, a merchant and mayor of Exeter. The facade is tall and jettied, culminating in a pair of gables. The top two floors have been over-restored but the first and second are more intact. The bay windows sit on timber brackets carved with lion masks and well endowed male and female figures. The friezes beneath them are decorated with black and white strap-work. During the 19th century No. 226 was home for the well known *Flying Post* newspaper, but in 1907 disaster struck when the ground floor was gutted to provide a new shop front and one of the friezes was chopped in half. Sadly, as in most of the High Street shops, antiquity is now only skin deep.

Nearly opposite are Nos. 41 and 42 (Laura Ashley), a similar pair of twin-gabled merchants' houses, which bear the date 1564, although their cellars of Heavitree stone incorporate part of the much older Close wall. Again the houses (now used as one) are tall and jettied out to gain maximum space from the narrow site, and they have oriel windows to obtain extra light. Their plans were simple: a front and rear room at each level, a newel staircase running up the middle, fireplaces in the stone side walls and a garderobe at the rear. During restoration in 1983 painted wall decorations were discovered depicting strap-work and figures in Tudor costume.

Possibly older than either of the above is No. 46 (Thorntons), a timber-framed house with a deep coving beneath the second-floor window and carved figures at the corners. The house has been restored but a picturesque irregularity survives. Numbers 45 (Pinder and Tuckwell) and 47 (Visionhire) either side are the same vintage, as investigation at the back makes clear, but they are now heavily disguised behind early 19th-century stuccoed fronts.

Across the road again, and representing the mid-17th century, is No. 227 (Austin Reed), one of the most spectacular sights in Exeter. It was built as a house for the merchant Simon Snow with at least twelve rooms on five floors, and, although today it is a modern shop, it retains most of its external features thanks to careful restoration in 1878. Comparison with its earlier neighbour is instructive, for in 227 classical features have begun to appear in a traditional timber-framed construction. The entire facade is more disciplined than in 225-226; columns with bases and capitals appear in the arcaded gallery on the third floor and a pedimented window is the main feature below. The building has been used as a shop for well over 200 years, and almost continuously by the clothing trade. In 1971 the ground and first floors were gutted and the covered walk created. Repainting in heraldic colours was last completed in 1986.

Several of the High Street shops have facades disguising much earlier buildings. An unusual example is No. 40 (Dorothy Perkins), which was given a brick facelift in about 1700. Described in the 1947 listing as 'very interesting' the facade is full of subtleties and elaborations. Setting off the brickwork is a stone cornice with ovolo moulding and stone quoins. The centre bay projects slightly and decorative brick panels alternate with sash windows, divided up by thick glazing bars. Such a carefully-proportioned building does not deserve the truly ghastly new shop-front on the ground floor. There are other 18th-century buildings in the High Street, but none so distinguished as No. 40. Number 200 has

38. Nos. 225-226, High Street.

39. No. 40, High Street.

40. High Street, with Lloyds Bank on the left.

an elegant frieze to the parapet illustrating the more delicate decorative effects popular by the end of the century.

The first half of the 19th century is represented by the stuccoed fronts and ponderous classical details of Nos. 206 (Edinburgh Woollen Mill) and 207 (Millets): heavy brackets and quoins and balustrade parapets. The second half of the century offers more varied and luxuriant features. Number 55 was built in 1883 for Wippells, a local firm with a national reputation as church furnishers and clerical outfitters. Appropriately, the style of the building is gothic revival, but the ground floor, which was built with a pair of pointed arch openings, has, once again, been cruelly defaced with a modern rectangular shop window. Next door, No. 56 is a typical late 19th-century brick building with ample florid detail and a shaped Dutch gable above an asymmetric facade. In the same genre, but even more extravagant, are Nos. 187-188 (Next) on the other side of the road, dated 1892. The niche in the gable of 188 once housed a 14th-century statue of St Peter, now preserved in the museum.

Changes to the High Street during the 20th century have been extensive and usually for the worse. Already in 1880, *The Builder* recorded some deplorable demolitions. In 1905 the street was widened at its southern end with a series of reconstructions, including a typically Edwardian baroque facade at Nos. 70-71 (Curtess Shoes) and an impressive bank palazzo at No. 59. Another bank, at No. 57, also espoused a weighty style, this time using Portland stone and self-confident Imperial classicism.

The classical style limped, exhausted, into the 1930s, No. 189-190 (MacDonalds) is a typically feeble essay of the type. More innovative is the moderne effect of the Chicago-style metal windows at No. 48 (Sherratt and Hughes). Then, on 4 May 1942, tragedy struck. The north end of the High Street was shattered by German bombs and a complete reconstruction seemed the only answer. The building line was pushed back on the west side to provide broad pavements and a fresh start was made in 1949 under the control of the City architect.

The result is typical post-war architecture in which neither the modern movement nor tradition plays a part. Instead a style best described as Post-War Civic was invented. It acknowledged equally the demands of austerity and a pride in the new era by dressing up rectangular blocks of shops and offices with expensive materials like polished granite walls, bronze doors or marble columns. Here and there an odd flourish, like a coat-of-arms, a balcony or a thin classical detail is randomly applied, but overall is an impression of dull solidity, like the institutions that do business here.

On the west side the bank buildings are the largest set pieces in a roughly symmetrical plan. Lloyds outdoes the others by flaunting green marble columns at the entrance and veneered panelling within. The east side adopts the same principle with Barclays providing the excuse for lavish use of Travertine marble cladding and an echoing circular banking hall. At the Bedford Street junction the bronze statue of the forlorn 11th Earl of Devon by E. B. Stephens (1880), brought here from the much lamented Bedford Circus, must wonder at the banality of it all.

HIGHER MARKET, QUEEN STREET

Paradoxically, although many regard the Higher Market as one of Exeter's finest buildings, its architect is virtually unknown, and its conception was in response to one of the worst disasters in the City's history.

In early 19th-century Exeter poverty and squalor were commonplace, whilst housing and drains were still essentially medieval. Calamity was inevitable and it came in the form of the cholera epidemic of 1832 during which 440 citizens died within two months. The

41. Higher Market, Queen Street.

authorities were belatedly galvanised into improving standards of public hygiene which included architectural competitions to design two new markets. That for the Higher Market was won by a Bristolian, George Dymond (1797-1835) who died tragically young before his masterpiece was realised. He was replaced by Charles Fowler who had won the other competition for the Lower Market (demolished in 1942).

Fowler (1792-1867) was Devon born, but he enjoyed a national reputation for his revolutionary use of cast iron and laminated timber, well in advance of any contemporary buildings in Europe or the U.S.A. He had recently completed the markets at Hungerford and Covent Garden and won the competition for building the new London Bridge. Naturally his Lower Market bristled with technological innovations and was distinguished by a coherent design which linked the interior to the facade. Dymond's market on the other hand was deeply conservative relying on the impact of the monumental Doric screen and portico, faced in Bath stone, which masked the unrelated market hall within which were stalls set between granite piers.

Originally the market served the fish, poultry, dairy and vegetable trades but by 1962 these had moved elsewhere and it closed down. Inevitably there were demands to demolish it but instead it became part of the busy Guildhall Shopping Centre, although not entirely unscathed. Six feet of plinth and steps at the southern end have been buried and the elegant iron railings removed. Inside, the pale green and orange paintwork has no classical precedent, but these are small criticisms compared to the vital preservation of the building itself.

38, HOLLOWAY STREET

Driving past this truncated stump of a house it is difficult to believe that behind the unprepossessing facade of blocked windows and toothed masonry there lurks the lovingly restored interior of old Larkbeare House, once a considerable medieval building, and, in the 18th century, the home of the Baring family. In 1819, however, the Barings moved out and a long period of decline followed. Much of the house was demolished as Roberts Road was developed and by 1975 the end seemed nigh when the remains attracted a dangerous structure notice. Fortunately the building was Listed and a public inquiry convened in 1977. The result was a triumph for conservation in the teeth of powerful opposition.

Listed building consent was refused and instead the Devon Historic Buildings Trust bought the house for £1 and set about raising money for the daunting task of restoration. It succeeded admirably as the interior now proves. The ground floor kitchen-living room is dominated by a massive moulded oak-beamed ceiling. On the first floor two bedrooms are dignified by more oak-timbered ceilings and original stonework, but best of all is the large three-bay room on the second floor with its original oak arch-braced roof. It is a tragedy that such handsome rooms are noisily hemmed in by busy roads and where a garden should be is only a commercial garage.

42. No. 38, Holloway Street.

HOLY TRINITY, SOUTH STREET

It is unfortunate that this shabby building should occupy such an important site in Exeter. The exterior is a crumbling patchwork of inept repairs, whilst the interior, occupied since 1977 by the White Ensign Club, is a textbook example of unsympathetic conversion.

A medieval church once stood on the site, adjacent to the City's notorious South Gate, but both were demolished in 1819. The present church replaced it in 1820, but

43. Holy Trinity church, South Street.

44. *Imperial Hotel*, New North Road.

it was not a happy time for ecclesiastical architecture, which was then much influenced by the desire to counter 'spiritual destitution' in the poorer suburbs. In 1818 the Incorporated Church Building Society was founded by earnest philanthropists for the purpose of erecting as many cheap churches as possible and Holy Trinity is a product of the Society's endeavours.

The architects were Robert Cornish and his son, another Robert, who were also the builders. They produced an unscholarly gothic revival style church, comprising four bays, a heavily castellated parapet and a west front dominated by pinnacles at each end and an octagonal belfry in the centre. It is not great architecture but it does have a naive charm that would be more apparent if the building was properly looked after.

The interior had a narthex, a nave with galleries and a minimal chancel, but it has been converted into a social club by fitting a false ceiling and using a great deal of mustard-coloured paint. Prominently displayed is a model of the cruiser H.M.S. *Exeter*, which was destroyed by enemy action in 1942. Holy Trinity was spared a similar fate during the Blitz but in retrospect it would have been a merciful release.

IMPERIAL HOTEL, NEW NORTH ROAD

When it was built at the beginning of the 19th century the *Imperial*, then known as 'Elmfield House', would have been a most desirable Georgian mansion surrounded by fields. Its plan was rectangular with dark red volcanic stone walls punctuated by six bays of sash windows facing the garden and three bays, including an Ionic columned porch, on the entrance front. Typically, for a house of the period, architectural detail was restrained and minimal: arched recesses around the ground floor windows, and a modest modillion cornice and recessed panels in the parapet. But such elegant simplicity has, needless to say, not survived the 20th century.

The first development was the introduction of the conservatory from Streatham Hall (*see* p. 117) by the then owner Dr. Heberden, an arthritis specialist and keen gardener. It is a barrel-vaulted structure built in reinforced concrete with vast fan-shaped windows at each end that radiate steel glazing bars. Now that only traces of Dr. Heberden's garden survive, the conservatory deserves mention merely for its curiosity value. Even that is lacking from the more recent brick extensions built to the north side for hotel accommodation. These make no effort to blend with the old house which surprisingly still merits a Grade II* Listed Building rating.

The interior of the house is equally disappointing as it is largely engulfed by hotel facilities. Some of the decorative plasterwork appears to date from the early 19th century, but not much else.

THE IRON BRIDGE, ST DAVID'S HILL

Exeter cannot compete with northern industrial towns when it comes to great monuments of 19th-century engineering. Its only contribution to the genre is the Iron Bridge, but this still serves its original purpose and looks as sturdy as ever after recent restoration, despite 150 years of use.

It was built in 1834 (20 years after its much smaller predecessor in The Close), with the object of crossing the Longbrook Valley. It has six arched spans, each 40 feet long, carrying a 24 foot wide road above. Add on the masonry approaches and the entire structure measures 800 feet. Each arch springs from a series of clustered columns with gothic quatrefoils in the spandrels. Above, a delicate balustrade also uses gothic forms which adapted so readily to engineering techniques. In raised letters on the first arch at each end the names of the builders appear: 'Russell and Brown' of Worcester, not far from Coalbrookdale where the first iron bridge in the world had been built in 1779. (Exeter's bridge was actually cast at

45. Iron Bridge, St David's Hill.

Blaina, Monmouthshire.) Section by section it was shipped to Exeter via the canal and then constructed at a cost of £9,000.

By the 1830s this type of bridge design was old-fashioned and it is intriguing to discover that a more daring, and much cheaper, suspension bridge was also proposed for the site. The first suspension bridge in England had been built over the River Tees in the 1740s and during the early part of the 19th century Thomas Telford and others had built many more. A scale model was constructed for Exeter's Improvement Commissioners to consider, but it was timidly rejected as a new and unproven design, just one year before Brunel's magnificent Clifton Suspension Bridge was completed!

ISCA ROAD

An Edwardian terrace of 42 flat-fronted, red-brick houses, ending in a classic urban view of a railway embankment. Nothing remarkable about that, one might think, save that these were the first council houses in Exeter, built under the provisions of the 1900 Housing of the Working Classes Act, and completed in 1907.

Despite their humble origins the houses were designed with some careful details – well-proportioned and panelled front doors with fanlight above and large mullioned windows with gently-arched lintels. Kitchens extend to the rear, and each house has a

46. Isca Road.

47. Livery Dole Almshouses, Heavitree Road.

garden. Inevitably changes will be made by new occupants, but even so the new glass panelled doors and aluminium windows are regrettable in these well-built, but modest, houses. The terrace has one other claim to fame: Nos. 1 to 8 were the first war-damaged houses to be rebuilt in Britain by apprentices.

LIVERY DOLE ALMSHOUSES, HEAVITREE ROAD

The almshouses and their elderly residents seem worlds away from the traffic which swirls all around them on what was once known as the Great Road to London. Even more remote is the time when public executions took place at a spot where vegetables now grow in productive cottage gardens. One of the last victims was Thomas Bennet, a Protestant heretic burnt at the stake in 1531 in the presence of the sheriff, Sir Thomas Dennis, whose family, as a belated act of penance, built the original 12 almshouses in the 1590s. They were rebuilt in Puginian medieval style in 1849 by Lord Rolle of Bicton and have recently (1980) doubled in size with the westward addition of more grey-brick houses.

Lord Rolle also restored the red sandstone chapel, first documented in the 1430s. It is a very simple aisleless building with dagger tracery in the east window, but otherwise notable only for the 17th-century altar rails and fragments of medieval glass introduced in 1849 from Bicton. It still serves its purpose ministering to the almshouse residents who each have two main rooms, one up, one down, for which they qualify after 10 years' residence in Exeter.

84, LONGBROOK STREET

Hampton Place, Castle Cottages, Park Place, Eldon Place – these are the quintessential names of early 19th-century terraces and they are all here in the southern half of Longbrook Street – pleasant brick houses with sash windows and fanlights over the doors. But amongst their well-regulated rows stands No. 84, a later architectural sport which has changed surprisingly little since it was illustrated by *Building News* in 1882.

The architect was Robert Medley Fulford (1845-1910), of Exeter, for his client Harry Hems, a prolific sculptor with an international reputation. Hems was born in Islington and apprenticed to a sculptor in Sheffield before returning to London and working on, amongst other buildings, the Foreign Office and the *Langham Hotel*. He then travelled to Italy to gain further experience, but two years later was forced to walk back to England, penniless. In 1866 he found work on Exeter's new Royal Albert Memorial Museum and, influenced by the discovery of a lucky horseshoe outside the railway station on his arrival, he decided to make Exeter his home. The omen proved right. By 1879 Hems had successfully chiselled his way over 400 churches and 100 public buildings. He needed a larger workshop and the Longbrook Street premises were the result.

Because Hems was particularly interested in gothic art his workshop, naturally, is gothic styled but with several peculiar additions. The ground-floor shop windows are divided by a pink Aberdeen granite column supporting the prophetic horseshoe on a shield and, overhead, the figure of Art herself, wielding calipers. On this upper floor Hems had his own studio – a singular little room. An exhortation is carved around the matchboard dado and above it, and surrounding the corner fireplace are some charming Delft tiles. Panels of stained glass, each depicting a flower, decorate the windows. On the second floor is another room with windows set in the apex of two arches surrounded by decorative leadwork and in the gable a circular opening incorporating the Hems' monogram.

Behind the facade are two brick chimney-stacks with a belfry between, followed by a buttressed wall and eight tiers of windows which light the three floors once occupied by the 100-strong workforce. Finally at the rear of the workshop is the timber yard and stores, still intact with the words *Vita brevis ars longa* boldly carved on a beam.

48. No. 84, Longbrook Street.

By the end of the century Hems was a well-known local figure and philanthropist. He lived next door to his workshop in a house distinguished by its corner turret. After his death his son built a new house, Hemsley, in the garden. It incorporates a length of medieval oak carving in the porch lintel. In 1938 the rest of the garden was built on by the Church of Christ Scientist.

LOWER CEMETERY, EXE STREET

It is a reflection on our irreligious age that cemeteries, in contrast to the more enlightened Victorian view of mortality, are usually ignored or, worse, despoiled, and Exeter's Lower Cemetery suffers like most others. This is especially regrettable since it enjoys a spectacular valley site in the centre of the city and is furnished with truly awesome Egyptian-inspired catacombs built into the hillside on the line of the old city walls.

The cemetery was opened in 1837, 200 years to the day after St Batholomew's Burial Ground, on the site of the old Franciscan Friary to the east, had been opened, in turn superseding the cathedral's own graveyard in the Close which, Oliver reported, was so full by the 17th century that it 'threatened to bury indecorously the very Cathedral'. The architect/builder was Henry Hooper, but no chapel or lodge was included in the specification. The Lower Cemetery itself spawned others in Whipton (1866) and Exwick Road (1877), but after some 17,000 interments it was closed in 1949. Most memorials have now been removed, the iron railings cut down and the dripping recesses of the catacombs are the haunt of cider drinkers and glue sniffers. Some evergreen planting survives, as does the gently-graded track for horse-drawn hearses, and beside it a few monuments with the inscriptions just discernible. Amongst the names of Exeter worthies are those of Samuel Wesley (1766-1837), the organist and composer, and John Gendall (d. 1865), the artist.

LOWER SUMMERLANDS

It is an ironic fact that much of Exeter which survived the Blitz has now been spoiled by inappropriate post-war alterations. This elegant well-proportioned terrace of double-fronted brick houses has escaped the worst excesses, but what a pity such details as missing railings and glazed front door panels are allowed. The coarse rebuilding of Nos. 5 and 6 (destroyed in 1942), with their clumsy concrete front paths and feeble reconstituted stone cornices, underlines slipshod modern methods compared to their infinitely more subtle original counterparts built by William Hooper in 1814.

The Blitz also accounted for Higher Summerlands, a much grander row of nine detached houses dating from 1804. It is a tragedy they were destroyed and the ugly police station replacement, erected in 1957, is no compensation whatever.

49. Lower Cemetery, Exe Street.

MAGDALEN ALMSHOUSES, DENMARK ROAD

These are the oldest of the dozen or so surviving almshouses in Exeter, dating from the 11th century. They were endowed by the church as a 'receptacle for lepers' who were cared for in a hospital near Bull Meadow until the mid-18th century. In 1863 the old houses were demolished and the present buildings erected in Denmark Road (named after Princess Alexandra of Denmark who married the Prince of Wales that year).

The houses form a symmetrical two-storey terrace built of Pocombe stone. They look as almshouses should: gothic windows and shadowy porches, dormers and barge-boarded eaves, a steep pitched roof and tall brick chimney stacks, all surrounded by a neat garden with spreading cedars. There are four varnished front doors within each porch giving access to four apartments, two upstairs and two down, each comprising two rooms. At the rear is a separate block, but similarly styled, of four apartments originally endowed in 1487 by John Palmer for poor widows.

MATFORD HOUSE, WONFORD ROAD

It is a pity that this Elizabethan house is not more accessible as it is one of the best of its kind in Exeter. It was built by Sir George Smyth, three times lord mayor, M.P. and the

50. Lower Summerlands.

51. Magdalen Almshouses, Denmark Road.

52. Matford House, Wonford Road.

richest man of his day in the city. The plan is typical, a central hall and screens passage with cross wings at each end; that to the east containing the domestic offices and to the west a parlour and living room. Bampfylde House in the Close had a similar arrangement (destroyed in 1942) and Cowick Barton (*see* p. 31) another.

Unusually for Exeter, Matford is built of cob, a cheap but time and space consuming material, and would have been thatched, a material outlawed in the inner city by 1600 because of the fire risk. Over the front door the plaster coat-of-arms is that of Elizabeth I, beneath, a spacious porch is entered past moulded jambs. The windows on this entrance front, like others in the house are replacements save two mullioned originals on the east wing.

The interior, according to published sources, includes that Devon speciality, early decorative plasterwork. The room over the hall features the Smyth coat of arms and fleur-de-lis ornament whilst in the south room of each wing the feet of some roof trusses are modelled with fluting and human figures.

MONT LE GRAND

53. Mont Le Grand.

The houses on the south side of this road form one of the grandest 19th-century terraces in Exeter and have recently received further acclaim as the beneficiaries of a most enterprising restoration project. They were built in 1840-1 for professional classes with large families and retinues of servants. The architectural style was still Regency classical but with detailing over-egged, as the Victorians preferred it. Particularly fanciful are the fanlights and the accompanying strips of window either side of the front doors.

By the 1920s houses of this size were less sought after, the professionals moved to smaller, detached homes in suburbia, and Mont Le Grand underwent conversion into flats and offices. It was the beginning of a downward spiral; within fifty years dry rot, vandals and squatters were active, especially in Nos. 6, 7 and 8, which were otherwise unoccupied. Then, in 1978, the terrace was included in a conservation area, which provided the impetus for Peter Hunt and Nigel Howe to buy these three houses and restore them, aided by a small grant from the city. It was a labour of love, 'for over two years the partners, their wives and families, lived in a perpetual shambles amongst the restoration work, with a professional day shift giving way to the D.I.Y. evening shift'. Luckily it has been worth it. Not only is the terrace itself preserved, but its example has encouraged others in the area to follow suit.

The opposite side of the street features contemporary houses on a similar scale and, in Bicton Place, larger detached houses, including a singular gothic villa so typical of its period.

NORTH STREET

Few streets in Exeter can match North Street's melancholy record of demolition, despite the antiquity of its buildings and its importance as one of the four main thoroughfares first planned by the Romans.

The blight began in 1769 with the loss of the medieval North Gate, the first of the four city gates to be razed, and with it the little church of St Cuthbert's. In 1878 a second medieval church, St Kerrian's, on the east side of the street, was demolished. According to Cossins, the street was widened in 1821, but more devastating was a second widening in the 1890s, when several early 17th-century houses on the west side had approximately eight feet shaved off them. The east side was not to be outdone, for as recently as 1972 its remaining timber-framed houses, including four listed buildings, were finally demolished. Rebuilding has been equally disastrous.

At the top of the hill the west side starts off with a vast swaggering late 19th-century shop and office block, brick built with all the fashionable attributes of the Flemish revival style piled on top. In comparison the brick facades of the remaining houses down the hill are very mean. They replaced the Tudor fronts lost in the 1890s road widening, leaving intriguing evidence behind them of timber-framed buildings. A stone-flagged passage next to No. 18 reveals a pegged timber-framed wall and moulded door jambs whilst at the back of the house carved brackets support an oriel window. A bomb in 1942 destroyed the stone kitchen building that once stood here, but traces of it remain. Inside the house, stone fireplaces and a 17th-century staircase also survive.

The 1970s rebuilding on the east side is catastrophic. Tall slabs of brick and concrete perforated with air-conditioning louvres are the unattractive backsides of large department stores. There is now no trace of the former shops, churches and pub, and the result is a street reduced to a one-way bolt-hole for motorists in search of a car park. In 1832 Exeter's devastating cholera epidemic broke out in North Street, but its long-term effects were insignificant compared to the destruction wrought by the planners 140 years later.

NORTHERNHAY GARDENS

This is a perfect evocation of Victorian Exeter. Here it was fashionable to promenade, listen to music from the bandstand, or admire the likeness of local worthies and art portrayed as sculpture.

54. North Street.

55. No. 18, North Street.

The contours of the park, following the hillside, were first created by the Romans, who quarried the volcanic trap stone for their new city wall, and later by the Normans who used the stone for their castle. In 1612 the formal gardens were first laid out for public use, but their present design, with a choice of paths, was prompted by the routeing of the London and South-West Railway along the valley floor in 1860, engendering another Victorian pastime – train spotting.

Today the gardens are well cared for and happily, after years of neglect, the barge-boarded lodges are being rehabilitated. Occupation of these will discourage vandalism, particularly to the statues which are tempting targets. Starting from the south entrance these are:

56. Northernhay, 'The Deer Stalker'.

1. John Dinham, 1866, by Edward B. Stephens, the Exeter-born sculptor. The seated stone figure is not very convincing. It was erected in memory of Dinham's 'Piety, integrity and charity', and ignores his more colourful career as silversmith, tea merchant and bankrupt.

2. Sir Thomas Acland, 1861. The standing stone figure has been damaged more than once. Acland, a Devon landowner and Tory M.P. for 40 years, was renowned for his philanthropic works.

3. The City War Memorial, 1921, by John Angel, a Newton Abbot-born sculptor, trained by Sir George Frampton. This is Exeter's most ambitious sculpture, comprising a 20-feet high granite pedestal on a cross plan surmounted by an heroic figure of Victory crushing a ferocious dragon underfoot. On each arm of the cross sits a bronze figure representing an aspect of war: a soldier 'In an attitude of triumph and repose', a sailor astride the hull of a ship, a V.A.D. nurse proffering a bandage and a muscular shackled P.O.W. Each is precisely detailed, and the whole tour de force cost over £6,000. Shortly after completing it Angel emigrated to the United States where he worked on the New York cathedrals of St Patrick and St John the Divine.

4. The National Volunteer Memorial, 1895, designed by Sidney Greenslade and executed by Harry Hems, both natives of Exeter. The base is plain grey granite but above it a fluted Portland stone column is decorated with every imaginable accretion. It commemorates Sir John Bucknill, M.D., F.R.S., who formed the country's first company of modern volunteers in Exeter in 1852. His portrait appears in bas relief.

57. Old Exe Bridge and St Edmund's church, New Bridge Street.

5. The Earl of Iddesleigh, 1880, by Sir Joseph Boehm. Another dull standing figure: Lord Iddesleigh, as Sir Stafford Northcote, was Chancellor of the Exchequer, 1874-80. A second portrait of him by Boehm graces the vestibule of the Palace of Westminster.

6. The Deer Stalker, 1878, by Edward Stephens. An energetic bronze commissioned by the city from the local sculptor. The stalker, who seems to wear a kilt, peers forward whilst restraining a large hound.

OLD EXE BRIDGE AND ST EDMUND'S, NEW BRIDGE STREET

Where else but in Exeter during the 1960s, a decade notorious for civic destruction of Blitz proportion, would an elegant Edwardian steel bridge be irretrievably broken up, the shady banks of the river beneath it ironed out between concrete barriers and the whole meshed into a cat's-cradle of busy roads? The one redeeming feature of this appalling muddle is the partially restored medieval bridge but this lies stranded and hidden to all save the determined pedestrian.

It was built in the 13th century, the brain-child of Walter Gervase, mayor of Exeter 1236-8, and possibly the third bridge on the site (the earliest was probably Roman and timber built). The Exe then meandered naturally through undrained marshes so that the bridge was about four times its present length and comprised 18 stone arches. Two of these form part of the crypt of the ruined St Edmund's church and five more are integrated within the area of the city brewery. Nevertheless, eight complete arches can still be clearly recognised, alternating pointed and round headed ribbed spans, some with chequered voussoirs.

The bridge was superseded by another in 1778, designed by Joseph Dixon and replaced again in 1904. In 1977 later accretions to the old bridge were removed prior to tidying up and furnishing with useful interpretative drawings.

St Edmund's church was contemporary with the bridge. It is a common dedication for bridge chapels since tradition relates that the Anglo-Saxon royal saint took refuge from the Danes under a bridge following the battle of Hoxne. In 1800 the tower was struck by lightning and the whole church rebuilt in 1834 by the Exeter architect Robert Cornish. This was condemned by Worth as 'totally deficient in architectural interest'. Only the ruin of the tower now survives.

PENNSYLVANIA CRESCENT

These five stuccoed villas with their own little triangular patch of pleasure ground must rate amongst the most desirable residences in central Exeter. They form a group dating from 1823, when fashion for the chaste Greek revival style was at its height, and have at their centre Crescent House with a three-bay facade loosely resembling a classical temple. It has a pediment and an acroterian at the apex, a broad entablature and incised pilaster columns. A short length of key pattern frieze and bay leaf wreaths on two capitals and around the attic oculus are the only concessions to frivolity.

The houses on either side are smaller, only two bays wide, much less 'correct' and more obviously Regency. They have no pediment, only wide eaves to hipped roofs and their vestigial pilasters are eclipsed by frothy ironwork supporting garden balconies. Only at No. 1, where the ironwork is missing, is the spell broken. It is an omission that should be put right if the Grade II listing of the houses carries any weight. Not so long ago new iron railings and a gate were made in key pattern style by Garton and King outside Crescent House to replace those lost in the war. It shows what can be done.

PENNSYLVANIA PARK

The terrace dominates the north-west skyline of the city although when it was built in a 10-acre field in 1823 it must have appeared uncomfortably exposed.

Eight houses were planned but only six built as a speculative venture by Joseph Sparkes, one of Exeter's many rich bankers who flourished during the 19th century. He was a Quaker who had bought the site in 1818, one hundred years after the death of William Penn, after whom the terrace was named. His architect was probably John Brown of Holloway Street, then employed on Baring Crescent where, as here, he introduced stucco into Exeter's architectural vocabulary.

The overall impression of the Park is one of refined proportions rather than architectural gimmicks. Broad eaves and delicate iron balconies are the principal features. In the 1890s the centre house was given a new porch and one has to admire such Victorian nerve, intoducing a baroque element into an otherwise symmetrical composition. Certainly it has quality, with oak panelling inside and sculpted Portland stone without.

That aside the terrace has survived remarkably unscathed despite the division of houses into flats. There are two small quibbles: first, the glazing bars in the windows are in disarray. Since the buildings are listed Grade II they ought to be put right. Second, the communal garden, such a crucial and picturesque foreground to the terrace, has seen better days. It would benefit by some tidying-up – just a little.

PINBROOK HOUSE, BEACON HILL

The date '1679' is above the front door thus identifying this building as a contemporary of the Customs House (*see* p. 31) and indeed the brick construction, large windows, broad eaves and hipped gables are common to both. The main difference, apart from its size, is that here there is evidence of blocked openings at each end of the front, down to floor levels, indicating there were once wings projecting from the main block, in fact two stubby staircase wings still project at the rear. Now, the most influential Restoration house was Clarendon House, Piccadilly, completed in 1667 for the Lord Chancellor, Edward Hyde, and also built of brick and with the same winged plan. Could this be the source?

Little is known of Pinbrook's later history. One theory suggests it was used as a garrison by Charles II's troops. In the 18th century it belonged to Sir John Elwill (but they are not his Arms above the front door) together with 1,200 acres. According to the 1840 tithe map,

58. Pennsylvania Crescent.

59. Pennsylvania Park.

60. Pinbrook House, Beacon Lane.

it was owned by Lady Fremantle, a daughter of Sir John, who let it as a farmhouse, and so it remained until the 1920s. After that it went into decline, due no doubt to encroachment by the city, and by 1976 it was derelict. Since then it has been restored as a home for the elderly although, by now, there is nothing of interest to be seen inside and the only 17th-century feature is a short length of stairs, encased in asbestos. Behind the house is the stable block, recently converted into housing.

THE PLAZA CENTRE, COWICK STREET

Here, on some ten acres of former marshland, is Exeter's most ambitious development of the 1980s, comprising three separate enterprises: The Plaza Leisure Centre, Sainsbury's Supermarket and, of more modest size, a branch library.

The architects were the Exeter office of Marshman, Warren and Taylor and their choice of building style was the fashionable post-modernism (that is, a mongrel style culled from others, particularly the classical, but executed in new materials to suit current needs and techniques), linked by a piazza (car park) and arcades.

The best of the three buildings is the library, which was built on the site of the St Thomas Bell Foundry, founded in the 16th century. It has a single pitch roof with a skylight running the length of the ridge, white rendered walls and angular projecting windows at each end. Details appear borrowed from 1930s seaside architecture: porthole windows, metal doors, bright blue paint and a curious art deco motif stuck on the railings. The interior, which is festooned with heating ducts and light fittings, is mainstream 1980s.

61. Plaza Centre, Cowick Street.

Sainsbury's is little more than a single storey brick warehouse flanked to the south by an arcade, apparently to mirror the craggy stone railway viaduct opposite, and a pair of pretentious arches to mark the supermarket doors. More glazed arcades lead through the car park, but few shoppers bother to make the detour to them and the result is chaos as pedestrians, shopping trolleys and cars compete against each other.

Finally there is the brashly-named Plaza itself, an £8,000,000 'Leisure Centre' opened by the Princess of Wales in 1986. It is dominated by the aptly-named 'fun pool' (no serious swimmer would dive in here), with its curved glazed wall closely copied from James Stirling's famous Stuttgart Art Gallery. The interior is worlds away from familiar old-fashioned Victorian baths. A welded tubular steel framework provides unrestrictive cover to an irregular shaped 35-metre pool and a host of other attractions for which shivering swimmers queue. The colour scheme, in pastel greys, blues and pinks, is interrupted here and there by harsh maroon. There are other sports facilities in the complex, linked together by glazed and galleried corridors. It will be interesting to see how the Plaza fares in, say, twenty years' time, but as a product of the 1980s it is unmistakable.

6 and 7 PRINCES SQUARE

Sir Nikolaus Pevsner observed that before the Blitz Exeter was largely a medieval city but after it, following the devastation of the old city centre, it became Georgian and early Victorian. What he ignored was the vast sprawl of later Victorian buildings, accounted for by the housing needs of an increasing population: 20,000 in 1801, double that in 1840 and about 50,000 at the end of the century. Most styles of domestic architecture are represented: from the grand terrace like that in Queen Street (*see* p. 73) to the modest artisan dwellings of Newtown (*see* p. 94).

In between the two extremes and representing a popular image of affluent, middle class Victorian housing is this pair of semi-detached houses. They must date from about the 1880s and their exteriors are largely unspoilt. By using brick the builder was able to vary shapes, colour and surface texture to indulge the High Victorian delight in ornament. Red is the dominant colour of the bricks, the cheapest and best, probably manufactured in Bridgwater or Wellington, but there are also bands of buff and black bricks for variety. Specially shaped rubbed bricks form the window arches and moulded brick courses surround the porch. These and the profusion of other details and materials were made possible by new modes of transport and manufacturing techniques. On the roof there are iron finials, crested ridge tiles and bands of light and dark slate; below there are large areas of plate-glass filling the bay windows and around the front doors bold acanthus capitals. Similar houses can be found all over Exeter and their quality makes the speculative housing of today appear very cheap and nasty.

PRINCESSHAY

A pedestrian street in both senses of the word; it was named by Princess Elizabeth, who performed the opening ceremony in 1949 during which she said: 'the centre of Exeter is something quite different and what rises here will be an example by which architecture and planning of our generation will be judged in years to come'. And so it is, for Princesshay is above all a reminder of those post-war years of utilitarian austerity when British architects timidly tried to catch up with the new movements of European architecture, but still indiscriminately persisted in adding frilly canopies, spindly balconies or bland sculpture when their nerve failed. In extremis they added flower beds which would distract from the buildings altogether. The concept was Thomas Sharp's, the town planner who drew up a scheme for rebuilding Exeter after the war. A 'feature' commemorative of the Blitz stands at the southern end of the street.

But there are two far worse blunders that underlie the history of Princesshay. Before 1942 Bedford Circus stood at its northern end. This was the finest of Exeter's late 18th-century building schemes and although gutted by bombs it was not irrevocably damaged. Despite that it was demolished and Princesshay substituted. At the southern end the Blitz cleared more buildings to reveal an uninterrupted view of the cathedral's Norman towers; at least Princesshay could act as a frame for these. Not so, incredibly, a bank was built to obscure half the view and thereby complete a thoroughly wretched episode in Exeter's architectural history.

THE PRISON, NEW NORTH ROAD

In the 18th century there were four prisons in Exeter, each catering for a separate category of prisoner. Conditions in all of them were disagreeable, but the worst was the notorious South Gate prison described by John Howard in 1791 as 'the same close, bad prison. Windows towards the street: no court: no water'. It was demolished in 1819 and a new City Prison replaced it on a site now occupied by the *Rougemont Hotel* (*see* p. 75) in Queen Street.

62. Nos. 6 and 7, Princes Square.

63. Princesshay.

It was designed by the younger Cornish (1788-1871) employing the continental radial system with three wings spreading from a single observation hub. Even so, by 1842 it was condemned as 'the very hotbed of vice' by a prison inspector although it was not demolished until 1863.

Meanwhile, on the site of an old jail in New North Road, a County Prison had been built between 1790 and 1794 following a plan by William Blackburn (1750-90), a friend of Howard and regarded by Pevsner as 'the most important early prison designer'. He had pioneered the radial plan prison in England at the end of the 18th century, but in Exeter designed only two brick wings with a governor's house in the centre. A stone lodge in front was also provided with a flat roof where the gallows could be erected when necessary.

64. The Prison, New North Road.

In 1810 Blackburn's prison was joined by a second, designed by another prison specialist, George Moneypenny. It had three wings and 'a noble gate of entrance 16 ft high and 8 ft wide, adorned with rustic cinctures and arch stones of uncommon grandeur, adopted from the design of the Earl of Burlington, as executed in the flanks of Burlington House, Piccadilly'. When both these prisons were replaced by the present building in 1853, this entrance block was retained and can still be seen.

The architect was John Hayward (*see* p. 79) who adopted the 'T'-shape plan with the entrance at the base of the upright. In addition to the three-storied wing, there were residences for the governor and chaplain at each side of the front and a chapel in the entrance wing. One hundred and ninety three cells were provided, each measuring 13 ft by

65. The Quay, the Wharfinger's house (left) and 17th-century warehouse.

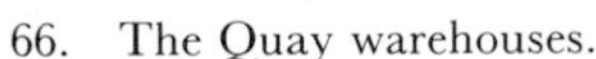

66. The Quay warehouses.

7 ft and paved with Delabole slate, while surrounding the entire site were walls that were over 20 ft high. These obscure much of the building, but the entire oppressive complex can be viewed from the vantage point of Northernhay Gardens.

THE QUAY

Historically this is one of the most interesting areas of the city, dating back to the Roman period, although the earliest surviving structure is now the 16th-century dock wall, excavated in 1986. Built above it is a late 17th-century warehouse (recently converted into the Quay House Interpretation Centre), which is the oldest building of its type in the country and unique in having a cantilevered awning that partially covered the moored boats. To the west is the Customs House (*see* p. 31), dating from about the same time, and the adjacent gabled wharfinger's office, built a hundred years later in 1778. To the east are two early 19th-century warehouses that dwarf their 17th-century predecessor.

The larger of them is built in red Heavitree stone, five storeys high and five bays wide, with broad pilasters between the openings beside which iron cranes would swing out to haul the cargo to and from the quay. The builders, and probably designers, were the Hooper family, in about 1835.

The other, built in 1834 of grey Pocombe limestone shipped direct from the Torquay area, bears a plaque with the name of the mayor in that year, de la Garde. The architect was Robert Cornish, the Younger. Until recently the massive ground floor doors and barred windows guarded exhibits from the Maritime Museum, established here in 1972, the catalyst for the rehabilitation of this previously depressed area, a transformation which is destined to continue among the decaying mills and warehouses of the old port.

Opposite the warehouses are two handsome gothic street lamps. They were made with four others by Macfarlanes the ironfounders of Glasgow for the Edwardian Exe Bridge, but dismantled in 1973 and replaced here in 1983, painted in the city's official colours of green and incorporating a part of its coat of arms on their base.

Finally, in recognition of the Quay's renaissance, the city spent nearly half a million pounds in 1988 to build the new 70-metre Cricklepit suspension bridge across the Exe. It is painted dark blue and, unlike the main Exe bridge, is very elegant. The designer was Dave Hubbard.

QUEEN STREET

Unlike other streets in the centre of Exeter, Queen Street was a late starter, laid out in 1835 to provide access to the Bristol to Exeter railway, the new North Road and turnpikes to Crediton and Barnstaple. Some of the best and worst of Exeter's 19th- and 20th-century buildings are here.

Beginning at the corner with High Street is the mixed blessing of Marks & Spencer, Nos. 2-8, rebuilt in 1980 after their predecessors were demolished due to structural problems. The Queen Street facade is a precast concrete copy of the 1837 original, which includes the old classical details, plus fibreglass reproductions of the Queen's statue, lions and unicorns. It is a laudable attempt but ruined by the inept lump that turns the corner, crudely detailed with ugly red bricks and massive concrete shafts that bear no relation to its neighbours in any particular. A cupola, salvaged from the old building, perches uneasily on top. The architects were Gundry Dyer. It is a wretched start to such a prominent street but perhaps not quite as bad as the brick and glass wall slabs of the C. & A. shop over the road which has rightly been described as appalling.

The next significant building on the south side is the Higher Market (*see* p. 48), which faces the old *Queen's Hotel* and a terrace of mid-19th-century stuccoed shops. These make

67. Queen Street, County Chambers.

68. Nos. 83/84, Queen Street.

an unremarkable group and the only building worthy of Dymond and Fowler's Market is their neighbour, Nos. 83-84. This was the central post office built in 1849 by W. H. & W. W. Hooper, and altered in 1864 when its use changed. It is a heavyweight classical building exuding all the self-confidence of the Victorian establishment from the vermiculated ground floor through the giant Corinthian order to the cornice and balustrade.

Still on the north side, the corner into Gandy Street is turned by an early 19th-century shop, No. 79, whose brickwork puts that at No. 2 to shame. Then follows the Royal Albert Memorial Museum (*see* p. 79) and its Italianate neighbour, the County Chambers, which makes a brave attempt to resemble a Renaissance palace. Its lavish detail and variety of materials is extraordinary: fanciful ironwork, bearded keystone masks, naturalistic botanical carving, grey limestone, yellow brick, marble colonnettes and paterae. It must date from the end of the 19th century and is unique in Exeter. The Dispensary opposite, helpfully dated 1840 on the foundation stone, designed by Samuel Greig, is a model of classical restraint in comparison.

Across Northernhay Street scale and style change again in the shape of the *Rougemont Hotel*, the greatest architectural muddle in Exeter. It was built on the site of the old city gaol as a railway hotel and completed in 1879 at a cost of £30,000. Clearly this was an insufficient sum for the architect, C. E. Ware, to do more than apply skin deep classical details to a nightmarish brick front that lacks any coherent design, and is now further compromised by a festoon of fire escapes. The interior is rather better in a ponderous way, reminiscent of a London club, with lots of columns and stodgy plaster ceilings. A stained-glass window on the stairs depicts a scene from Richard III. Predictably it is by the Exeter glass-maker Frederick Drake.

Directly opposite is Central Station, rebuilt in 1933 and now serving the Southern Region railway. Two curved brick wings meet at the booking office block in the centre, performing a dreary essay in the Queen Anne revival style. The only feature with charm is the cupola, in the Wren tradition.

At the south-west end of Queen Street, high above the Longbrook valley, the tempo alters once more with Nos. 44-53, a grand mid-19th-century stucco terrace. It was built following the cholera epidemic which devastated central Exeter in 1832 and is one of several terraces developed at that time on green field sites away from the seat of infection. Bystock and Queen's Terrace include gabled houses with gothic detail, Richmond Road is gabled and classical but the symmetrical, classical facade of the Queen Street terrace is much more ambitious than any of these. It comprises a centre block four storeys high and three storey wings either side linked to pedimented three bay blocks at each end. Together with the later 19th-century terraces in Victoria Park Road in St Leonard's they represent the best examples of their type in the city.

69. Queen Street Clocktower.

QUEEN STREET CLOCKTOWER

The proper title for this anachronistic landmark is 'The Miles Memorial Drinking Fountain and Clock Tower'. William Miles was a retired army officer, city magistrate and philanthropist. In 1877 his concern for the welfare of carriage horses inspired him to build a granite watertrough marked by an obelisk at this busy crossroads. On his death in 1881 his widow decided to build something far grander to commemorate both her husband and Queen Victoria's forthcoming Diamond Jubilee. She commissioned a local architect, T. A. Andrews, who replaced the obelisk with this splendidly eccentric monument.

The plinth is in red sandstone with four grey limestone clustered columns, bracketed out at the corners. A bronze inscription and two fighting bulls mark the Queen Street side, a text from the *Book of Proverbs*, the Miles' coat-of-arms and a door leading to an internal iron ladder fill the other three. At the head of the plinth, where scrolls and arches melt into one another, the corners are embellished with groups of winged sea horses. A convex-sided limestone shaft, bounded by colonnettes, rises from the plinth to support the clock, which has finials at each corner and an octagonal cupola above.

The architectural style throughout is a free mixture of baroque with a dash of art nouveau which completely eclipses the surviving humble water trough at the base.

RENSLADE HOUSE, EXE BRIDGE

Happily, Exeter was largely spared the brutal intrusion of tower blocks, those architectural dinosaurs of the 1960s and early 70s. There are a few exceptions and the three main culprits, noticeable in most views of the city, are Debenhams (1964) at the corner of Sidwell Street and New North Road (but its future is currently under discussion), Exeter College on Hele

70. Renslade House, Exe Bridge.

Road, designed by the city architect H. B. Rowe in 1963 and, worst of all, Renslade House which dominates the approach to the city over the Exe bridge. It was built in 1971 at a cost of three-quarters of a million pounds and betrays all the worst features of its kind: the wrong materials – concrete and glass, the wrong colour – green, the wrong shape – concave block and convex podium, and above all, the wrong scale – a 10-storey monster. Significantly perhaps, the developer responsible for this disaster was himself seven feet tall and he employed architects from out of town, G. W. Mills and Associates of Bromley, Kent.

ROUGEMONT CASTLE, CASTLE STREET

Exeter's castle has played an important and varied role in civic life for over 900 years so it is a pity that its present judicial function precludes greater accessibility, especially to the walls which command splendid views of the city.

It comprises two distinct parts: the medieval fortifications and the later court buildings. The former were first built in about 1070 by Baldwin Fitzgilbert, a distant kinsman of William the Conqueror, on the volcanic mound within the north angle of the city walls. He dug a great earthwork to carry the curtain wall, strengthened by a towering keep-gatehouse at the southern corner. This was constructed in a local red-coloured basalt, hence the castle's name 'Rougemont', which also qualifies it as the earliest stone castle in Britain.

A description of domestic arrangements within the gatehouse is lacking, but Oliver suggested:

> A strong square building of five storeys. The lowermost consisted of dungeons for the confinement of captives and state prisoners; the second contained the stores; the third served the accommodation of the garrison; the fourth were the best apartments for the Governor and his family; and the uppermost was portioned off for chambers.

Architectural details were old-fashioned; typically pre-Norman are the triangular-headed windows and herring-bone stonework inside the curtain walls. These appear to have been strengthened in the 12th century and probably the flanking towers were also built following the three-month siege successfully mounted by King Stephen.

Traditionally the castle was the venue for a court and in 1607 a Sessions House was built in the inner bailey. This was demolished with other buildings in 1773 to make way for the present limestone Palladian-style courthouse, 'a large, plain and convenient building'.

The architect was Philip Stowey of Exeter who had designed more elaborate decorations only to have them eliminated by James Wyatt, acting as adviser to the cost-conscious authorities. The building was enlarged by three brick bays to the west in 1895, for the use of the newly-formed County Council, and a neo-Palladian wing to the east in 1905.

The forecourt is overlooked by E. B. Stephens' statue of the second Lord Fortescue. Few will now remember that in 1814, as a young Devon member of parliament, he met Napoleon, later publishing the subject of their conversations in a book; nor that in 1886 the first hot-air balloon ascent in Exeter was made here by Monsieur St Croix; nor that this was the first site of the Devon County Show, and, where lawyers now walk so purposefully beneath the portico, was the venue for the sheep-shearing competition.

ROUGEMONT HOUSE, NORTHERNHAY PLACE

When this house was first built in the 1770s by John Patch, a distinguished surgeon at the Royal Devon and Exeter Hospital, it would have resembled a brick box on three floors, but after his death it was bought by Edmund Granger, a wine merchant, who modernised it in about 1810. It was he who added the distinctive ground floor bow windows, the canopied balcony above, a new Tuscan porch and stucco on the walls which together transformed

71. Rougemont Castle, Castle Street.

72. Rougemont House, Northernhay Place.

the 18th-century house into an unmistakably Regency villa. He also landscaped the garden within the castle moat which still provides an ideal sylvan environment.

In 1910 the city bought the house from Richard Somers Gard (*see* below), since when it has served as a school, a library and as part of the city museum. So many changes of use have left their mark, none more so than the adaptation of the interior in 1987 to a costume museum with all the attendant paraphernalia necessary to protect the fragile textiles. Only the black and white paved entrance hall escapes division by glazed screens which separate visitors from the eight other period rooms and their precious exhibits. The Adam style fireplace in the drawing room came from the old Exeter School in the High Street (*see* p. 35) destroyed in the Blitz. Not on show are the brick cisterns that are curious survivors from the original house, fitted into the basement to collect water piped from valley gutters in the roof. The only known comparable example occurs in Marisco House, on Lundy Island, where it is still in use.

ROYAL ALBERT MEMORIAL MUSEUM, QUEEN STREET

Nineteenth-century parish churches excepted, the High Victorian gothic revival had little impact on Exeter, save in one notably exotic flowering – the museum. Inspiration for the building came from Richard Somers Gard, an Exeter M.P. who donated the Queen Street site, and an architectural competition which attracted 24 entries, including the winner John Hayward (1808-91). Hayward's architectural antecedents were sound: a relation by marriage to Charles Barry, and the designer of two important Exeter buildings – the prison and St Luke's College – besides a number of churches.

The museum foundation stone was laid in 1865 and after delays caused by a strike and shortage of funds, the building was completed in 1870. In its inception it was the equivalent of a 20th-century arts centre, a most fitting tribute to the polymath Prince whose death in

73. Royal Albert Memorial Museum, Queen Street.

1861 prompted its creation. The ground floor housed the museum, classrooms, a reading room and the city library. Upstairs was more of the museum and the art school. Over the next 30 years two additions were required to cope with such various needs in a style borrowed from North Italian gothic (1894 by Medley Fulford; 1898 by Tait and Harvey), but despite these the Queen Street facade creates the greatest impression.

Its gothic style relies partly on 13th-century French models and partly on the influence of John Ruskin. Hayward encouraged his sculptor to study French medieval sculpture in Normandy. He also put 'a valuable library at his disposal' and this may have included Ruskin's influential *The Seven Lamps of Architecture*, published in 1849, in which he stressed the importance of 'sculpture and colour', precepts which influenced a generation of architects and were exemplified in the museum.

To achieve colour Hayward turned to geology. Thus, the basement and entrance arcade piers are Chudleigh limestone, the columns pink Aberdeen granite and the walls mainly purplish Pocombe trapstone with bands of limestone. The windows are dressed with Bath stone and divided by colonnettes of red sandstone from Bishop's Lydeard. Add to this a richly-sculpted surface on several planes and what would otherwise be an ordinary symmetrical design appears very complex.

Inside the hall are columns of black Devon marble which support the best of the carved capitals. Ahead is an imperial staircase with walls resplendent in red, blue and gold paint. At the half-landing a statue of Prince Albert by E. B. Stephens presides. So far so good, but from here on the conception fades beneath the weight of contemporary exhibition trappings: white paint, dusty false ceilings and ugly cases. This is unfortunate because the galleries retain many of their original features; marble fireplaces, iron barley-sugar columns, a hammerbeam roof and polychrome voussoirs to the doors. With a little imagination and a lot of paint the interior of the museum could be a visual extravaganza that would complement its exterior as well as providing a new lease of life for tired exhibits. (Basement contents include old fragments of Holloway Street, Bamfylde Street and Bartholomew Street houses.)

THE ROYAL DEVON AND EXETER HOSPITAL, SOUTHERNHAY

Except for Sir Christopher Wren's Chelsea and Greenwich Hospitals, which were reserved for the armed forces, the 'modern' hospital in England was an 18th-century phenomenon. The first was Westminster, 1719, followed by Guys, 1724, St George's, 1733, the Bristol Royal Infirmary, 1735, and in 1736, Winchester, founded by an energetic young clergyman, Dr. Alured Clarke (1696-1742). Five years later he became Dean of Exeter and, 'although the hand of death was upon him at the time', promptly set about repairing the deanery (*see* p. 32), and founding the Devon and Exeter Hospital. Untroubled by 20th-century red tape, the hospital's 'foundation stone was laid in a very solemn manner . . . and a party of soldiers saluted with three volleys of small arms', just 35 days after the inaugural meeting. The first patients were admitted in 1743 and by 1748 the hospital had 100 beds.

The original building was the first large Georgian building in Exeter comprising a central brick block with wings either side. Like other hospitals of its time it was architecturally domestic in character with a minimum of detail: in this case only a cupola, quoins and plat bands (the centre pedimented three bays were moved forward later in 1772).

The architect and builder was a Devonian, John Richards (1690-1778), who generously provided his services free. He had started life as an apprentice joiner, married his master's widow at the age of 20, subsequently turned to architecture and later became a surveyor and valuer. Unhappily, towards the end of his life he became completely insane.

74. Royal Devon and Exeter Hospital, Southernhay.

As with all hospitals, expansion and modernisation have been regular occurrences so that, with the exception of the panelled boardroom, nothing substantial remains internally of the original and today the entire building is used for administration. The additions have all been brick built and none is very distinguished. The Halford Wing at right angles to the 18th-century block was the first, built 1854-6 with the architect John Hayward acting as adviser. The gothic chapel followed in 1868, financed by Arthur Kempe, a surgeon. It was the best of the additions, but demolished in 1975. In 1895-6 the dour Victoria Wing designed by local architect Charles Cole was built parallel to Halford to which fashionable sun balconies were added in 1933. E. H. Harbottle's Victory Wing for nurses was built to the rear in 1920 and finally Leslie Moore's (1883-1957) unadorned and well-proportioned out-patients' pathology department was linked to the south of the 18th-century block in 1935-7.

SACRED HEART ROMAN CATHOLIC CHURCH, SOUTH STREET

Leonard Stokes (1858-1925) was perhaps the most eminent Catholic architect at the end of the 19th century. He had trained under two of the most celebrated High Victorians, G. E. Street and G. F. Bodley, before setting up practice on his own in 1883, and this is his first church, jointly executed with the local architect, Charles Ware.

In 1952, a time when Victorian buildings were little appreciated, Nikolaus Pevsner pronounced the church 'not worthy' of Stokes, and certainly the exterior, which suffers from

75. Sacred Heart church, South Street.

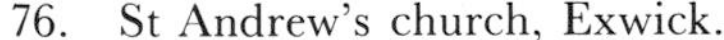

76. St Andrew's church, Exwick.

a cramped sloping site, is unremarkable. Only the west end is easily visible, with its pair of attenuated gothic windows, a stumpy tower, completed in 1926, and an awkward narthex extension. But the interior is far better, helped by lavish Edwardian fittings and a rich variety of building stone.

As befits a Catholic church the plan derives from French, not English, gothic sources. It has an apsidal east end, vestigial transepts and a lofty nave comprising only an arcade and a geometric traceried clerestory. The octagonal columns and interior walls are built of veined purple coloured Pocombe stone with Bath stone dressings. The chancel arch piers are of Corsham and Portland stone. Beer stone, which is easily worked, was used for the stylish pinnacled reredos and side altars, designed by the Reverend Alexander Scoles of Bridgwater. The high altar itself was replaced in 1906 and made of alabaster and green marble. It stands on an elaborate parquetry floor that would look more at home in Italy. On the walls either side are large murals depicting Christ the High Priest and James Tuberville, the last Catholic bishop of Exeter. Oak choir stalls, designed by Ware in 1913, were installed in memory of Edward Petre, a young airman killed in 1912 whilst attempting a flight from Brooklands to Edinburgh. Finally, the stained glass is all 20th century, much of it made by Frederick Drake, a local craftsman. One window frame, on the staircase leading to the choir loft, is older than the rest. It was re-used from the 15th-century *Bear Inn*, previously the town house of the Abbots of Tavistock which formerly occupied this site.

ST ANDREW'S CHURCH, STATION ROAD, EXWICK

Exwick developed as a railway village in the 1840s when Brunel's G.W.R. reached Exeter and a church, initially a chapel of ease to St Thomas, was an essential element. The foundation stone was laid in 1841 with two familiar local names carved on it: J. W. Buller of Downes, who performed the ceremony, and John Hayward, the architect. His was a simple, early Decorated style building, comprising three bays in the nave and a chancel, which from outside looks much like any other small Victorian church. The interior, however, is more rewarding, thanks to the munificence of William Gibbs, a high church enthusiast, who in 1873 transformed this church, like so many others (*see* p. 97).

First it was enlarged by adding a vestry and a north aisle set behind limestone columns with floral carved capitals by Hems, but it was the redecoration that really mattered. In the chancel the stained-glass window by W. Wailes was complemented by a mosaic reredos, an angelic frieze stencilled on the walls, and ceiling panels painted with angels, saints and the fruits and seasons of the earth. The new aisle and the nave ceilings, tie beams and king posts were also polychrome stencilled. The only casualties are the light fittings, which are nasty modern replacements, and a dreary carpet that covers the red patterned tiles before the altar.

ST ANNE'S ALMSHOUSES, SIDWELL STREET

This site, framed in the angle between the Old Tiverton and Bristol roads, once provided a convenient location for a medieval hermitage to which was added the present chapel in 1418. It was dedicated to St Anne, the patron saint of weavers, in recognition of the many weavers who then worked in St Sidwell's parish. After the dissolution of the monasteries in 1539, the Mainwaring family became the owners and they endowed almshouses here for eight poor people. These were restored in 1838 and again in 1907, when two new brick and half-timbered houses replaced four originals. Their date is on the iron rain-water hoppers which also show signs of Arts and Crafts detail with fleurs-de-lis and rosettes. The architect was W. D. Caroë.

The chapel, traditionally built in Heavitree stone, has a three-light Perpendicular window

77. St Anne's Almshouses, Sidwell Street.

78. St Catherine's Almshouses and Annuellars College, Catherine Street.

in the east wall and a pair of niche canopies either side which perhaps once shielded statues of the Virgin Mary and St Anne. Above is a timber-ribbed barrel vault. It is a tiny building, surrounded by shops and traffic far removed from Byzantium until, in recent years, it became the centre of worship for the Greek Orthodox Church. Today a flimsy iconostasis divides the chapel, and the exotic rites are regularly performed amid the icons, the smell of incense and the ringing of bells.

ST CATHERINE'S ALMSHOUSES AND THE ANNUELLARS COLLEGE, CATHERINE STREET

Excavations during 1987-8 in this central Exeter location not unexpectedly revealed an architectural palimpsest. The earliest structure found was part of the rampart and ditch thrown up by Roman legionaries after their capture of what was then a British village in the first century A.D. Later, after the town expanded and stone walls were built, a Roman courtyard house replaced the earth defences in about the fourth century. A floor mosaic with geometric patterns was retrieved from this period. Then, with the advent of the cathedral, the site bordered St Catherine's gate to the Close and a gate to a Dominican friary, now replaced by the post office. In due course the Roman house disappeared and a medieval replacement with a hall built towards the Close followed. A cathedral chancellor is recorded living here in the 13th century and this may have been his house.

In about 1440 Canon John Stevens endowed the north half of the property for use as an almshouse for the benefit of 13 old men. It comprised a chapel, a refectory, and cells for the inmates built around a small courtyard. The kitchen fireplace, part of the exterior walls to the cells and the roofless chapel survive. Nearly a century later the southern half of the medieval house was converted into the kitchen and buttery of the Annuellars College (*see* p. 19). Two large Heavitree stone fireplaces and the foundations of the triple door openings from the buttery to the hall remain.

The site is now ruinous as a result of the Blitz but even before 1942 changes had occurred. The Annuellars were disbanded in 1548 and their hall eventually became part pub and part clubhouse. The almshouses ended life as the labour home of the Church Army. After the war it was decided to preserve the shattered old buildings as a memorial to that horrific event in Exeter's history but in the process further demolition took place under the pretext of tidying up. Restoration in 1988 was more sensitive.

ST DAVID'S CHURCH, QUEEN'S TERRACE

Despite its youth, St David's must rate as the most distinguished of Exeter's parish churches as well as an Edwardian church of national importance. It is probably the fourth building on the site (the earliest was Anglo-Saxon), replacing an early 19th-century Greek revival church by the county surveyor, James Green. That church, once described as barn-like and, in common with many of its contemporaries, having galleries fitted across the windows, was so gloomy that winter evensong could start no later than 3.30 p.m. Members of the fashionable congregation did not care for such old-fashioned inconveniences, nor were they amused by the impressive sight of St Michael's, newly-risen to the south-east, which had poached several of their number.

Preliminary discussions about rebuilding were held in 1882 but nothing was done until the energetic Mr. Valpy-French was appointed rector in 1894. Encouraged by him a limited architectural competition was mounted, presided over by the elderly church architect, James Brooks, who had no hesitation in selecting W. D. Caroë's design from the five submitted.

Caroë was an experienced architect who had worked with J. L. Pearson on Truro cathedral in the 1880s and was undaunted by the particular constrictions of the St David's site which

79. St David's church, Queen's Terrace.

was limited to the prescribed area of its demolished predecessor. Following Pearson's example at St Augustine's, Kilburn, and several other late Victorian churches, Caroë made the most of the available space by building buttresses within the walls and piercing them to form ambulatory aisles.

The impression made by St David's today is of a complex grouping dominated by its tower articulated by deep membranous buttresses and details finely carved in distinctive Bath stone. The interior is spacious and both architecture and furnishings display a rare consistency and quality. This was not achieved without a long financial struggle and indebtedness to the Thornton West family who paid for over half the £18,000 cost. The building style is a fluid gothic Perpendicular, not uncommon in the late 19th century. Mouldings tend to merge imperceptibly into walls whilst sinuous leafy forms worked in wood, stone and metal betray the influence of art nouveau. Before even entering the church the high standard of craftsmanship is evident in the unusual iron door handles. Such refinements reach a climax in the inlaid marble sanctuary floor and the carved reredos.

ST DAVID'S STATION, BONHAY ROAD

The first station was built in 1844 to serve the western end of I. K. Brunel's Bristol to Exeter line and, after its inauguration, attended by Brunel himself, life in Exeter was never the same again. Previously the journey to London had taken 25 hours by stage coach, now it took under five, including stops, in the world's first and fastest express train. The station, designed by Devonian Francis Fox (1818-1914) was also remarkable. It was covered by a single span pitched roof, 360 feet long and 132 feet wide, the widest of its kind in Britain.

In 1864 a new station was built to counter the competition set by the London & South Western Line's Queen Street terminus. Henry Lloyd of Bristol designed a lavish Westleigh

80. St David's Station, Bonhay Road.

stone facade dressed with Bath stone and punctuated by niches and round-headed windows. The parapet was decorated by a guilloche border and once topped with 25 urns. The urns have gone but the facade remains, now partially hidden behind a further facelift of 1938-9 built in Bath stone, 11 feet wider than its predecessor and with the G.W.R. initials prominently displayed.

By 1938 Fox's train shed had already disappeared after a major reorganisation in 1912-14 when new platform buildings and valanced awnings were erected. However, since 1940, apart from the ticket office and cafeteria, refurbished in 1984, St David's has been relatively unchanged. It is still possible to enjoy tiled direction signs, a 'Refreshment Room, Snack Bar and Dining Room' fascia and, best of all, a commodious G.W.R. waiting room with varnished furniture and faded photogaphs of Devon's tourist attractions. It is an extraordinary anachronism that instantly conjures up nostalgia for steam trains and seaside holidays.

ST KATHERINE'S PRIORY, ST KATHERINE'S ROAD

This large two-storey 13th-century building is a most unexpected find, sandwiched between a railway line and dense 19th-century suburban housing. In fact it was once the west range of a cloister to a medieval nunnery whose abbey church formed the north side where now there are houses in Prince Charles Road.

Records suggest the nunnery was the resort of aristocratic ladies, who enjoyed a convent régime that was far from onerous, but like other abbeys their religious life was curtailed at the Dissolution. By the beginning of the 17th century the church was ruinous and the remaining guest house wing owes its survival to its adaptation into a dwelling and later a farmhouse. In 1933 its existence was again threatened when housing development engulfed the farm land but at the same time its importance was recognised, the site was excavated and the building partially restored. In 1982 it was converted into a local community centre.

The building now stands alone in a field with the remains of an old cob wall and a few stumps of outlying masonry, the only other evidence of its monastic history. The exterior stonework bears the scars of countless alterations. A new roof and casement windows were built in 1862, and again in 1982, when the lavatory block was added to the south end. These are barely acceptable; what is not are the yellow plaster infills on the west facade, part of the 1980s alterations which feebly baulked at the additional cost of using matching red Heavitree stone.

The interior has to withstand a rigorous programme of community use which is reflected in haphazard furnishings and some lack of respect for its architectural features. Fortunately these are solidly built and have survived, so far. On the ground floor there was probably a cellarium and outer parlour; above, once reached by a staircase on the outside, was a hall and parlour. The three-bay hall was screened at the south end by an oak service partition of four two-centred arches comparable with only one other example from this early date, in Suffolk. At its other end is the parlour, possibly the prioress's own room, made comfortable by a 13th-century fireplace with colonettes in the jambs and decorated with two sculpted corbel heads at ceiling height. She also enjoyed the privilege of her own garderobe built within the corner of the turret.

ST LEONARD'S CHURCH, ST LEONARD'S AVENUE

The impact of this church is created by the enthusiasm of its packed congregations who sing songs, not hymns, and listen to preachers wired up for sound wearing baseball caps and using a variety of visual aids. Architecture takes second place.

In fact the present building is probably the fourth on the site; its immediate predecessor by Andrew Patey was less than 50 years old when it was demolished and replaced by S. Robinson's robust gothic design, aided by John Hayward junior, later supervised by his pupil Medley Fulford (*see* p. 55), The foundation stone was laid by the Earl of Northbrook, a member of the Baring family, who also contributed funds as a thanksgiving for his safe return from India where he had been Viceroy. Then in 1881 Mrs. L. A. Miles, of Dix's Field, paid for the fine tower and spire, designed by John Tarring, a favourite architect among evangelicals. A lavish brass memorial records Mrs. Miles's gift in memory of her husband (*see* p. 75). The latest addition of a lavatory, kitchen and foyer block built in 1968 without regard to the gothic style makes a sorry comparison with these Victorian extravagances.

The church interior is plain and robust: a segmental apse, nave and aisles with arcade piers of alternating red granite and octagonal stone.

ST LOYE'S CHAPEL, RIFFORD ROAD, HEAVITREE

The origins of this little building are obscure – 14th-century documentary evidence suggests it was the chapel attached to a medieval mansion, known as St Loye's, which was demolished

81. St Katherine's Priory, St Katherine's Road.

82. St Leonard's church, St Leonard's Avenue.

in 1838, whilst the architectural evidence of the three splayed lancet windows in the south wall dates its construction from the 13th century. Certainly its antiquity is unchallenged and hence its survival, albeit roofless, minus its north wall and surrounded by a council estate.

Jenkins, writing in 1806, recalls it had a chancel, but when Charles Worthy examined the building nearly a century later this had gone and the north wall had been replaced in cob. One hundred years further on and this too has collapsed, as cob will if exposed to rain, which accounts for the mound of earth now visible inside the chapel.

Protective railings now surround it, crouching like an exotic but mangy animal in a zoo, occasionally peered at and sometimes abused. To avoid a sad end to an already sorry saga, the building urgently needs a new purpose. There must be many it could fulfil for local residents as it would be kinder to adapt it than wait for the inevitable collapse. In 1987 plans were laid to restore the chapel, convert it into a centre for a new housing development and carry out an archaeological dig. At the time of writing nothing has been done.

ST LUKE'S COLLEGE, HEAVITREE ROAD

Old photographs of St Luke's reveal groups of athletic young men posing in creeper festooned gothic cloisters rather like an American ivy-league college. But this is only a vision of the old St Luke's, built at a cost of £7,000 between 1853 and 1854 to the design of the Exeter architect, John Hayward (1805-91) (*see* p. 79). Since then the romantic image has been steadily eroded by later additions and alterations, not least the removal of the ivy.

In 1911-12 expansion began with new buildings by James Jerman, including enlargement of the chapel, and continued in 1934-8 with the addition of the brick Haighton block on the east side of the green, named after a college benefactor. In 1942 bombs damaged the Hayward wing which was repaired in 1947, but without the gothic windows, and any pretence to antiquity was finally expelled in 1967 when the brick and concrete south-west wing of study bedrooms was built adjacent to a new dining hall nicknamed the 'giraffe house' on account of its being top lit by a series of vaulted skylights. The extent of these changes is reflected in the number of students accommodated: in 1854 there were 40, now there are over seven hundred.

ST MARTIN'S CHURCH, CATHEDRAL CLOSE

Typically of the medieval churches in the centre of Exeter, St Martin's is a tiny, cramped and ancient building. It was probably consecrated in 1065, three years before the Normans established themselves in the West Country, and it still shows traces of Anglo-Saxon long and short work although the church was largely rebuilt with Heavitree stone in the 15th century. Today the dominant exterior features are the Perpendicular west window and the tower added in 1675.

The problem of the awkward site is clearly visible inside the church: the axis of the chancel is different to the nave, with an east wall not at right angles to it, there is only space for one stubby transept and the few windows are set high up the walls. The furnishings date from the turn of the 17th and 18th centuries. They include a panelled gallery at the west end, painted with the royal coat of arms flanked by those of Bishop Trelawney (1688-1707) and the city of Exeter; box pews; a pulpit and an exceptional chancel ensemble. The altar is enclosed by a turned oak balustrade and the walls fitted with benches where communicants would sit, rather than kneel as was the low church custom. The stone reredos has lost the text of the Ten Commandments, the Creed and the Lord's Prayer, but the coat of arms surviving on its right-hand side is that of the Hooper family, one of several wealthy

83. St Loye's chapel, Rifford Road.

84. St Luke's College, Heavitree Road.

85. St Martin's church, Cathedral Close.

86. St Mary Arches church, Mary Arches Street.

families who worshipped here. The exuberant monument on the chancel north wall commemorates Philip Hooper who died in 1715, *ex hac civitate mercator*, shown wearing a full-bottomed wig. A later equally fine wall monument in the transept depicts the sentimental image of a soul, in this case Elisa Mortimer's, died 1826, being guided to heaven by an angel. The sculptor was the Bristolian Edward Baily (1789-1867).

These monuments have been carefully preserved, even if some of the new paint colours are rather modern, but on the whole St Martin's is unusual in Exeter for its sensitive conservation. An object lesson is the west window which by the 1970s had reached a state of collapse. A recommendation to replace it was, fortunately, rejected in favour of a careful repair which succeeded in preserving three-quarters of the original fabric.

ST MARY ARCHES CHURCH, MARY ARCHES STREET

It is ironic that this, the only church in Devon with complete Norman arcades either side of the nave and once regarded as Exeter's most attractive parish church, should now be cluttered up as an information centre (since 1983). The aisles are filled with massive bookcases, the old inscribed floor slabs lie hidden beneath carpet tiles and a new interior porch, office and exhibition screens obliterate the west end.

That the four-bay, scallop capital arcade survives at all is a miracle. Alterations in the 15th century included new aisles and windows and the west tower reduced in size. In the 17th century Puritan re-ordering caused the removal of old furnishings and stained glass. A new reredos, altar rails, box pews and two-decker pulpit were introduced at the end of the century only to be badly damaged in 1942 when a bomb removed the 15th-century wagon roof. Of the furnishings only the reredos and altar rails survived. Fortunately many of the fine 16th- and 17th-century memorials commemorating local worthies, including several mayors, notably Burnet Patch, also escaped damage.

In 1950 the church was restored by S. Dykes-Bower. Using timbers from an American landing craft which saw action on D-Day, a new barrel vault was built but the truly awful appearance of the exterior with crude new imitation stone and pointing to match is unforgivable.

ST MARY STEPS CHURCH, WEST STREET

St Mary's is Exeter's most familiar parish church, thanks to its picturesque situation and unusual tower clock. It survives, just, on the edge of the city's spaghetti junction amid a group of half-timbered houses and is famous for its painted clock face. This illustrates the seasons in the four spandrels beneath two swarthy jacks, which probably date from the 17th century. The central seated figure holding a sceptre might represent Henry VIII, but for generations the tableau has been nicknamed 'Matthew the Miller and his two sons', commemorating an especially punctual local resident.

The earlier 12th-century St Mary's was rebuilt of Heavitree stone in the 15th century. Its steeply sloping site necessitated a vaulted undercroft with the church above reached by a short staircase. The nave is a simple rectangle with a south aisle beyond an arcade of broad depressed arches. Over both are sealed wagon roofs painted blue and pink during the 1960s restoration when a new east window was also inserted. The stained-glass artist was John Hayward, who depicted Christ surrounded by the four symbols of the Evangelists. The radiating fragments of glass are Expressionist in style with pale colours unmistakeably of the period.

As the church has no monuments the Norman font commands attention. It is a cylindrical monolith carved with bold abstract patterns and a band of rough foliage ornament. The chancel screen is the only other feature. The south aisle section was brought here from the

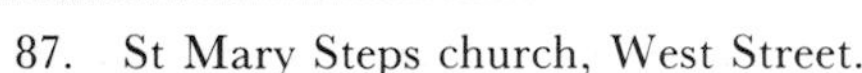

87. St Mary Steps church, West Street.

88. St Matthew's church, Lower Summerlands.

medieval St Mary Major in the Cathedral Close, following demolition of that church in 1865. St Mary Steps was undergoing restoration at the same time, apparently master-minded by the rector himself who saved the screen but then enlisted an inexpert parishioner to repaint it, thereby destroying much of its charm. The nave screen was built as part of the 1860s restoration of the church by Edmund Ashworth, carved, predictably, by Harry Hems who also made the font cover and altar.

ST MATTHEW'S CHURCH, LOWER SUMMERLANDS AND NEWTOWN

Clifton Road, Clifton Street, Chute Street, Albert Street, Sandford Walk, East John Street and Portland Street are the nucleus of Newtown – each lined with 19th-century terraced houses that would look more at home in a northern industrial town than Exeter. Some, which are tiny and flat-fronted, were built in the 1830s, most later in the century on land that was once a nursery garden. By 1880 there were some six hundred houses here. In 1942 the area was blitzed but surprisingly, and to the city's credit, the survivors were modernised and the roads partially pedestrianised so that the close-knit identity of the community remains.

When the area was first planned the usual amenities were included: corner shops, pubs, schools. Boyd's almshouses and of course a church, St Matthew's by Medley Fulford, whose design was chosen in 1880 in competition with six others. It is a traditional gothic building described as 'a simple composition in the Geometrical Style having double transepts not of great projection . . .'. It should have cost £6,000 but, despite being mainly brick built, this figure was exceeded and economies made. The chancel was added in a second phase and the west tower never started. Inside, the furnishings were 'convenient rather than beautiful' and they lack the reredos and screen originally proposed. The overall impression is rather gloomy due to a cavernous dark-stained pine vault, austere brick walls, a plum-coloured tiled dado and grey granite columns. The carved acanthus capitals by Luscombes the builders are the only relieving features. St Matthew's was designed to seat 900 but of course never has and probably never will.

ST MICHAEL'S CHURCH, CHURCH ROAD, ALPHINGTON

Alphington is now an Exeter satellite swamped by a vast industrial estate and decimated by busy roads to south Devon. Miraculously, some fragments of what was a pretty village survive: Regency villas, an 18th-century terrace, a rectory dated 1609, some cob-walled thatched houses and, at the centre, St Michael's, a fine building surrounded by mature trees and a survivor of two terrible disasters. In 1826 four bell ringers were injured and one killed when the tower was struck by lightning. In 1986 a glue-sniffing arsonist set light to the roof causing over £400,000 worth of damage. Despite that, as triumphant testimony both to the faith of its congregation and to the art of the restorers, Gundry Dyer the architects and Herbert Read the wood carvers, both Exeter firms, St Michael's re-opened for worship within a year and despite these misfortunes remains one of Exeter's most interesting churches.

The exterior is typically Devonian Perpendicular in style. It has a well buttressed, stately west tower, aisles north and south and large Perpendicular windows. Entrance is through the two-storeyed north porch where an ancient notice asks 'please take off your pattens', those wooden predecessors to the wellington boot.

Inside, the church is dominated by a majestic vaulted 15th-century screen with the usual row of badly-painted saints along the panelled base. It faces a barbaric looking early 17th-century screen within the tower arch made up from panels taken from the west gallery and crudely painted with armorials. The nave piers between the two ripple with sharply-defined mouldings and each supports oversized capitals studded with angels. Spanning everything is the restored arch-braced pine roof still charred in places and exuding an acrid scent. The chancel was worst affected by the fire so its entire roof has been rebuilt and the painted bosses restored. It was also the part of the church most affected by John Hayward and Son's restoration in 1884, so here the walls are stencilled red and green, the floor is tiled and an extraordinary flamboyant reredos, featuring St Michael, betrays the confident hand of Harry Hems (*see* p. 56).

Wall memorials in the aisles are both baroque and neo-classical, the former unabashed by reference to mortality with a death's head, the latter more obliquely with a veiled urn. A series of unusual Doulton tile plaques dating from the early 20th century appear on the window cills of the south aisle. Finally, there is the Beer stone font. This is one of the finest Norman fonts in the county and it was sufficiently well known to be copied in the 19th

89. St Michael's church, Church Road, Alphington.

90. St Michael's church, Dinham Road.

century for the Temple Church in London. It is carved with interlaced arcading beneath a vine scroll border inhabited by hunters and animals, hardly a baptismal subject, but medieval sculptors were never that fastidious.

ST MICHAEL'S CHURCH, DINHAM ROAD

The builder of this enormous church was William Gibbs, a wealthy merchant who lived near Bristol. His family, which came from Exeter, had made a fortune importing guano and nitrates from South America for use as fertilisers. In 1842 William succeeded as head of the firm and until his death in 1875 profits from the noxious trade averaged £80,000 to £100,000 per annum. It was a lot of money, but a passion for building linked with deeply religious convictions enabled him to spend it without guilt.

His extravagances began with the purchase of a country estate at Tyntesfield, Somerset, where he remodelled the house and later added a chapel. Having established himself there he turned next to churches, commissioning only the best gothic architects for his new building projects. First, in 1856, Sir Gilbert Scott designed St Mary's, Flaxley, Gloucestershire; in 1867 it was Rhode Hawkins at St Michael's, Dinham Road; in 1868 G. E. Street at St Mary's, Paddington, and in the same year William Butterfield at Keble College Chapel which cost a fabulous £50,000, and finally Scott again was responsible for a major restoration of Exeter cathedral, all funded by Gibbs.

St Michael's, Dinham Road, cost a more modest £20,000, but this was still enough to create the largest and most sumptuously decorated of Exeter's churches and, according to *The Builder* in 1872, 'the point of attraction in modern architecture'. Hawkins (1820-84) was architect to the Committee of the Council of Education for 31 years, and as such designed many schools, but when released from this mundane occupation his work could be ostentatious, not least at St Michael's.

The spire is 220 feet tall, the roof vault 65 feet and the architectural style based on correct late 13th-century 'geometric' adorned with an exceptional array of naturalistic sculpture by Hurley, a Taunton sculptor, above columns of Devon marble. The chancel was also brilliantly decorated with stencilling and stained glass by a local man, Frederick Drake, furnished later with a reredos by W. D. Caroë and the high altar by Herbert Read.

Gibbs' own memorial, a recumbent effigy against the north wall of the chancel, was made by H. H. Armstead, R.A. Today he would be saddened to witness the decline of his church, whose palatial size has become a major liability. The Anglo-Catholic ritual no longer attracts the number of worshippers Gibbs envisaged. The transepts are not in use and the chancel decoration is disappearing beneath the damp and dirt – even a church guidebook for this important Exeter landmark is beyond the means of the tiny congregation.

To the south-west of the church, fulfilling the role of a cathedral close, are Bishop Blackall's Charity School and four rows of semi-detached gabled brick cottages known as Mount Dinham. Twenty-four were built in 1861; 62 by John Dinham, a successful Exeter grocer and jeweller, eight by John Scanes and eight by the citizens of Exeter for 'reduced tradesmen' rent free. Entrance into the mercifully traffic-free drive is between two wellingtonias, and beyond the fountain at the far end is a tremendous view over the Exe Valley. It is a spectacular site and a classic example of Victorian philanthropy which has survived more or less intact. Beside one of the houses is a small concrete structure labelled 'No. 99'. This is the last surviving air-raid shelter in Exeter.

ST MICHAEL'S CHURCH, CHURCH STREET, HEAVITREE

The present church is Victorian but it occupies an ancient site, probably chosen by the Anglo-Saxons when a vast parish circumscribing the entire city was formed. What the earlier

91. St Michael's church, Church Street, Heavitree.

buildings looked like is unknown, but in the 15th century a new St Michael's was built of Heavitree stone with a nave of six bays with richly-carved angels and foliated voussoirs. By 1844 this building was again too small and the stone decayed, so it was demolished and replaced by the present larger gothic style church with limestone walls but retaining the old Beer stone arcade and windows. The architect was David Mackintosh. To commemorate Queen Victoria's Golden Jubilee in 1887, a new limestone tower was added, designed by the diocesan surveyor, Edward Harbottle, who went on to enlarge the gabled chancel in 1893.

That is the church as it used to be, really rather dull save for the 15th-century remnants incorporated within it – but in 1939 that changed when, at total variance with accepted artistic opinion, a reredos by Sir Gilbert Scott was rescued from the cathedral, where it had never been universally admired, and hurriedly re-erected at St Michael's which it now dominates. It depicts the Transfiguration, Ascension and Ascent of Christ's Spirit at Pentecost and had been designed by Scott in 1874 amidst great controversy. Originally it was refused admission into the cathedral until the Court of Arches, the supreme ecclesiastical court, overruled the objectors in what was known as *The Exeter Reredos Case*. In 1988 restoration of the alabaster figures and semi-precious stones revealed its exuberant colour and intricacy that only the High Victorians would have had the courage to design. It makes a visit to St Michael's well worthwhile.

ST MICHAEL'S CHURCH, CHURCH LANE, PINHOE

It is a Christian tradition to dedicate churches on high ground to St Michael and Pinhoe is no exception. The first church on this site dated from before the Conquest, since when the village moved down the hill to become a dreary suburb of Exeter leaving the church high and dry in a gloriously isolated position.

The present building was begun in the 15th century and is now host to a patina of lichen and climbing roses. It stands in a picturesque churchyard entered through a thatched 17th-century lychgate and enhanced by a medieval granite preaching cross before the south door and a glimpse of the former brick vicarage to the west (built in 1703 after its predecessor was destroyed in a hurricane, and surely one of the most attractive and least-known houses in Exeter).

The embattled tower of the church itself is stocky and buttressed in the Devonian fashion, the nave windows are Perpendicular and the late 19th-century restoration of the chancel is tactfully discreet. Inside, the dominant feature is another Devonian speciality, a splendid

92. St Michael's church, Church Lane, Pinhoe.

carved 16th-century oak screen. It was probably installed at the same time that the church was enlarged with the north aisle. Before the Reformation it supported a platform on which stood the rood, accessible from the staircase in the south wall. Unfortunately the screen's coloured decoration is lost, but paint does dimly survive on the contemporary pulpit where the arms of Bishop Cotton (1598-1621) and the Bampfylde family overlie figures of saints. There is more fine medieval woodwork on three oak bench ends in the nave (one of them carved with a winged figure of the Archangel Michael overpowering Satan, the dragon), and in the roof bosses, which feature crowned and whimpled faces gazing down and, at the south-west corner, an irreverent figure sticking out his tongue, Maori fashion. In 1700 another figure was carved, in elm, and now stands by the south door. It represents the parish beadle, in 18th-century costume, collecting for the poor. It was restored by the ubiquitous Harry Hems and is a great rarity. There remains one other treasure to see; a rugged stone font hatched with chevron patterns around the bowl in the unaffected style that only a Norman mason would carve.

ST NICHOLAS' PRIORY, THE MINT

This Benedictine priory was the only important monastic foundation in Exeter and one of only three founded by the irreverent William Rufus. Like most of its kind, it suffered at the Dissolution when only a fragment was left standing and that too has not survived unscathed in the intervening 450 years. It has served as private house, tenements, workshop, warehouse, parish room, and, since 1916, museum. The result is an architectural puzzle until some concept of the original monastic plan is grasped.

The present building once stood parallel to the western cloister walk, now the route of the Mint which divorces it from the surviving frater building sited north of the cloisters. Everything else to the south-east, including the priory church, has disappeared and the materials used to rebuild part of the old Exe Bridge and the city walls.

Entrance to the museum is now via the Tudor room, distinguished by the 16th-century moulded plaster ceiling, one of the earliest to survive in Exeter. The original panelling has gone, an omission partly made good by the introduction of a curiously-carved 17th-century panel depicting the Judgment of Paris brought from 195 High Street. Equally curious is a case of architectural trifles used as a reference collection by the sculptor Harry Hems. To the right is the door to the great kitchen, a high-ceilinged room, thoroughly restored and furnished with an eclectic assortment of kitchen utensils and furniture. Only the north fireplace and ceiling beams appear authentically medieval.

Of far greater antiquity and interest is the Norman undercroft south of the Tudor room, with crude rib vaults supported on two ponderous stubby columns. Such massive architecture dates unmistakably from the 11th century and is typical of any Romanesque building in western Europe at that time.

The next two rooms are small and dark, their original purpose unknown. Possibly they housed stores, just as now they house a rag-bag of ecclesiastical paraphernalia that includes clocks, bells and carved masonry. The nine Purbeck marble twin capitals of waterleaf shape, a design Pevsner suggests was introduced by the Cistercians at Roche Abbey in Yorkshire *c.* 1170, once supported a circular planned lavatory that stood in the cloister garth. Circular lavatories are rare – Canterbury, Durham, Lewes and Much Wenlock are the only other known English examples.

On the first floor the character of the building changes to the comfortable living quarters of a late medieval prior. There is a large hall sub-divided by a typical screen arrangement and roof braced with collarbeams. Following secularisation, exotic black and white painted arabesques were introduced as decoration to the walls and window reveals. The bedroom beyond, furnished with what appear to be museum rejects, extends into a charming little oratory.

This much is open to the public, restored by a local architect, Lewis Tonar, under the direction of Harold Brakespear. Not open are the second floor, comprising servants' rooms, and the remains of the frater and undercroft the other side of the Mint. In the garden is a weather-beaten Saxon cross shaft incised with meandering patterns. It had been used as a cut-water on the Exe Bridge in the 16th century and was brought here for a well-earned retirement.

ST OLAVE'S CHURCH, FORE STREET

Hugger-mugger in the city centre, Exeter's old churches offer unexpected surprises; one moment the visitor is in the midst of a busy street, the next in the peace of a medieval interior. At St Olave's on the verge of Fore Street, the contrast is particularly marked. It is also, in common with its fellows, an unassuming little building as well as a foundation of great antiquity, in this case by the Saxon Gytha, mother of King Harold who died at the

93. St Nicholas' Priory, The Mint.

94. St Olave's church, Fore Street.

95. St Pancras' church, Waterbeer Street.

battle of Hastings. It is claimed that Saxon long and short work can be seen at the north-west corner of the nave and perhaps survives within the tower but, again like its fellows, St Olave's has been altered many times since the 11th century and one cannot be sure.

The most enduring of the changes occurred in the late 14th century when the church was substantially rebuilt with the addition of a north aisle, separated from the nave by octagonal piers. A lively, but damaged, sculpture panel depicting the scourging of Christ survives from this period, now fixed within the tower. In the 15th century, when Exeter was one of the largest and wealthiest cities in the country another north aisle was built and large Perpendicular-style windows inserted throughout. The proximity of other buildings probably precluded further expansion and in the 17th century St Olave's experienced a period of decline but revived following the Revocation of the Edict of Nantes in 1685 when it was set aside for refugee French Huguenots whose tomb slabs pave the floor.

A new improvement phase began, inevitably, during the 19th century. In 1815 the south aisle was moved out to engulf the tower and provide space for a gallery, part of which remains. Further restoration in 1875 included refurnishing and the provision of the present font and pulpit. Finally, in 1902, the polychrome reredos and the gothic style screen were installed.

ST PANCRAS' CHURCH, WATERBEER STREET

Swallowed up in the modern Guildhall shopping precinct is the church of St Pancras: small, intimate and very ancient. Nearby redevelopment work in the 1970s revealed a Roman pavement and it has been suggested St Pancras may qualify as one of the earliest Christian sites in Britain. In their time the Saxons built here; three Saxon fragments found in the 19th century are embedded in the south chancel wall, including a vigorous grotesque head, and the church is documented in the 12th century although only the font, a robust cylinder with a single band of pellet decoration beween mouldings, survives from that period. The nave and chancel now date from the 13th century with some 16th-century rectangular windows and a late medieval timber wagon roof.

St Pancras has always lived cheek by jowl with neighbouring buildings, hence the blocked west window. In 1806 it was described as 'dark and gloomy . . . and may soon be desecrated'. Instead in 1831 the cathedral surveyor, Robert Cornish, restored it and further restoration followed in 1888. J. L. Pearson, architect of Truro cathedral and then working on Exeter cathedral's cloisters, built a new chancel arch and fitted the Y-tracery east window. Following the last war further tidying up took place and in the 1970s a floor more suited to a kitchen than a church was laid, but despite all this St Pancras has survived. Miraculously it retains an atmosphere of tranquillity which most other central Exeter parish churches have lost and it serves as a constant reproach against arid post-war development in Exeter represented by the Precinct that surrounds it (by Norman Jones and Rigby, 1969-76).

ST PETROCK'S CHURCH, HIGH STREET

In 1951 Pevsner noted the plan of St Petrock's was 'among the most confusing of any church in the whole of England' on account of the change in orientation from the medieval north-east/south-west to the Victorian south-east/north-west, with several intermediate stages besides. It is typical of a city church on a cramped site to develop piecemeal in this way, and a useful engraved brass plaque in the present chancel charts the changes and their dates.

The story begins with the original chancel and nave, followed by the south aisle of 1413, a second in 1513 (column capitals sporting sizeable angels), and third in 1587. In 1828 another south aisle enlargement was designed by Charles Hedgeland of Exeter who also sealed over the vaults and provided roof lights, whilst the old chancel was furnished with a typical Georgian reredos of Decalogue and Lord's Prayer by 'Mr. Davey'. Finally, in 1881 Messrs. Hayward of Exeter turned the old chancel into a baptistry and added the new one with oak fittings, much to the annoyance of Beatrix Cresswell who considered the church was 'stripped . . . of all architectural merit'. This is not so, but it is true that the church is now more Georgian and Victorian than medieval.

96. St Petrock's church, High Street.

Although the parish was always small it was also wealthy and can therefore boast several good monuments, particularly the 17th-century Hooper family wall memorial bearing portrait busts of William and Mary Hooper, painted in sombre colours. More gaudy is the extraordinary frieze of 32 tiled Victorian and Edwardian memorials round the nave. Most were covered by oak panels in 1951 when this exuberant work was less appreciated than now, but such prissiness is unacceptable and the panels should be removed without further ado.

Better known is the Ivie memorial under the tower. It depicts the Last Judgment, executed in 1717 by the Exeter sculptor John Weston (fl. 1696-1733) and brought here from St Kerrian's when that church was demolished. Rupert Gunnis, the historian of British sculpture, wrote of Weston, 'all his monuments are important' and considered this was the equal at least of any contemporary work in London. High praise indeed!

ST STEPHEN'S CHURCH, HIGH STREET

Once there were 33 medieval churches in Exeter's city centre; now there are six grouped into a single central parish with St Stephen's the hub. It is a venerable inheritance and all the more reason to deplore the current treatment of this church where drastic reordering of the interior has been conducted, seemingly oblivious to the fabric of a building whose history dates back to before the Conquest.

A church on the site is mentioned in the Domesday Survey and when excavations took place in 1826 and 1865 arches and four columns of a Saxon crypt were discovered. The church was probably rebuilt in the 13th century, destroyed by fire in the 17th and rebuilt in Heavitree stone in 1664. In 1826 Joseph Rowe, fresh from building Pennsylvania Park, remodelled it yet again in neo-gothic style. Miraculously it survived the Blitz which devastated most of the High Street, only to suffer the most insensitive rearrangement of the interior in 1972. All the pews were removed and the eastern arches, which opened into a raised chapel under which runs a narrow lane, were blocked. The plan was to provide unfettered space for coffee mornings, flag days, concerts and so on, all very laudable but the result is ghastly. Fake parquet flooring, plastic stacking chairs, white gloss paint, bathroom heaters and spindly pendulous lights prevail. The building is hardly recognisable as a church since everything else has been stripped out save a few fine 17th- and 18th-century wall monuments which seem to gaze incredulously down at such an act of crass barbarity. St Stephen's deserves better than this.

97. St Stephen's church, High Street.

98. St Thomas' church, Cowick Street.

ST THOMAS' CHURCH, COWICK STREET

The parish church of St Thomas has an eventful history but now finds the 20th century heavy going, being plagued by vandals and dry rot whilst attracting only small congregations.

Its earliest predecessor was built near the west end of the medieval Exe bridge in 1261 and survived until flood damage caused its removal to the present site in 1412. Relics of these two buildings are the inner door of the south porch, reputedly from the first church, and the arcade piers from the second. During the Civil War that church was burned down and most of what one sees today dates from the re-building of 1657, costing £597, and 19th-century additions and restorations.

The north aisle dates from about 1810 and the gaunt gabled chancel and transepts were tacked on by Andrew Patey in 1829. These represent that attenuated gothic style common to the period. In 1872 and 1909 early 19th-century box pews and galleries were removed. Bombing in 1942 damaged the east end, destroyed the stained glass (replaced in 1951), and the reredos by John Bacon (1777-1859). An effigy by Bacon does however survive. It lies recumbent in a gothic niche in the north wall of the chancel to commemorate the death of his daughter in 1842. It was extravagantly praised by *The Ecclesiolgist*: 'It is not too much to say that few of the best ages of Christian art surpass it', although perhaps today the great blackened wooden eagle lectern, apparently the oldest in the country, is more appreciated. It was brought here from the cathedral and stands on a tripod base guarded by fierce carved dogs. The font was installed by John Medley (vicar 1836-45) who in 1841 founded the Exeter Diocesan Architectural Society which was committed to both High Anglican worship and High Gothic architecture.

St Thomas's has one other claim to fame. During the Prayer Book Rebellion in 1549 the vicar unwisely sided with the rebels and paid for his belief with his life. His corpse

> having been brought to the foot of the tower, was drawn to the top by a rope and there hanged in chains upon a gallows which had been erected on its summit. He was arrayed in his vestments, and a holy bucket, a sacred bell, a sprinkler and a pair of beads were suspended around him. According to the barbarous custom of those days the body was tarred over and remained suspended from the gallows during the remainder of the reign of Edward VI.

Another minor curiosity is the memorial cross placed outside the north aisle. It commemorates the heroic lifeboat rescue by Grace Darling of 'nine human beings . . . off Northumberland' in 1838 and was placed here by an admiring congregation in 1845.

ST THOMAS' STATION, COWICK STREET

In 1965 the Victorian Society compiled a list of the sixty railway stations in England and Wales most worthy of preservation. St Thomas' was amongst them, but 20 years later it was a scene of pigeon-haunted desolation, until rescued in the nick of time by a new leisure and shopping development.

The present station dates from 1861 when it was rebuilt as the first stop on the South Devon railway out of St David's. The line was then broad gauge, with trains propelled by Brunel's ill-fated atmospheric system. Because the line crossed Cowick Street it was raised on a viaduct and the station provided with two storeys. This gives it stature which is reinforced by the well-proportioned arcaded stuccoed facade in the Italianate style. A glazed cantilevered canopy shelters the approach.

The ground floor is now a bar but the arcading of the exterior is repeated inside and has fortunately survived a brash conversion job. Upstairs is better. The open timber roof with massive king posts and struts satisfyingly overwhelms the new restaurant. Originally a similar timber span extended over both platforms and the railway itself. This has gone and

99. St Thomas' Station, Cowick Street.

it is ironic that the only part of the refurbishment that fails is the station platform itself. Mean concrete bunkers have replaced the daring timber roof and the place is rubbish-strewn and clearly neglected. It is a pity that some of the care lavished elsewhere in the building has not been directed here.

SALMON POOL LANE

These neo-Georgian semi-detached houses are 50 years old, but it is a tribute to their builders that they still look good today. They were designed by Louis de Soissons (1890-1962), a Canadian-born architect who had achieved fame with his plans for Welwyn Garden City. There he came into contact with the builder, A. E. Malbon, who subsequently moved to Devon to take charge of Staverton Builders Ltd., the company set up to develop the Dartington Estate in the 1930s. The association between the two endured and de Soissons worked on several Devon projects with Staverton Builders, including Salmon Pool Lane. In the garden suburb tradition the houses are well built – the graded Cornish slates appear especially solid. All but one have an asymmetrically placed, gabled bay with an upstairs Venetian window and the woodwork is painted white throughout. Each has a front garden behind trim privet hedges and exudes the solid comforts and precise habits of middle-class life: Atcoed outside and Hoovered within.

It is a great pity that the development did not cross the road. The garish 1960s semis opposite represent all that is cheap and nasty in post-war architecture.

100. Salmon Pool Lane.

101. Shilhay, Commercial Road.

SHILHAY, COMMERCIAL ROAD

This estate is built on land once occupied by the medieval woollen industry and without doubt is the most attractive of Exeter's post-war council housing developments. It was designed in 1979 by the local office of architects Marshman, Warren and Taylor and comprises approximately 150 homes planned in groups around several courtyards each bearing a name borrowed from the cloth trade: Fuller, Weaver, Dyer and so on. Some are for family use but most are for old people and the design reflects this. (The proximity of the river was considered a danger to children.) Throughout the estate, courtyards are kept private and casual parking discouraged. The scale of the housing is modest; it includes flats and maisonnettes, nowhere more than four storeys high, using a local red brick and grey concrete tiles whilst avoiding monotony by an apparently random variety of heights, widths and windows.

Detail too is carefully worked out; T.V. aerials are hidden and there are no tarmacadam driveways but paved and brick surfaces leading to garages inconspicuously embodied in the design. Several are now creeper covered as the planting matures. Add to that an enviable site landscaped to overlook a green sward by the river and it is no wonder that Shilhay was given a design award gold medal.

SIDWELL STREET METHODIST CHURCH

The pioneers of ferro-concrete construction were Frenchmen who in the 1880s and '90s developed a technique which combined great versatility with low cost. One of their most striking buildings was the parish church of Saint Jean de Montmartre, built in Paris in 1894, where free interpretation of the gothic style was achieved by using thin interlacing concrete arches, later acknowledged by the historian Henry-Russell Hitchcock as 'epoch making'.

The engineer responsible for this construction was Paul Cottancin who became internationally known for his cheap and daring work which he patented. The system in-

102. Sidwell Street Methodist church.

103. No. 67, South Street.

104. Southernhay.

volved a network of steel wires on which hollow red bricks were fitted and subsequently set in place and filled with concrete. Decorative details, precast in moulds, were also made of concrete and threaded on the wires.

In 1902 Cottancin had not yet built in Britain, but that year Exeter architect Frederick Commin sought contractors for his newly-designed Sidwell Street church and Cottancin's tender of £9,000 (£1,000 less than his competitors), was irresistible. In fact it may have been his undoing for Cottancin went bankrupt during building and the church demonstrates none of the Parisian bravura, being hidden instead behind a conventional Edwardian baroque facade. Only the interior of the dome, still showing evidence of a rough concrete skin, and the cantilevered gallery hint at the unusual construction. The furnishings, added later, are more reminiscent of a lavish Edwardian pub or hotel foyer, with a pair of swooping staircases either side of a massive polished oak reading desk hemmed in by characteristically floral-patterned stained glass.

SOUTH STREET

It is shocking to learn that half South Street was destroyed in the Blitz and depressing to witness the drab brick replacement shops now lining both sides. They were built between 1954 and 1961 when the street was widened causing yet more demolitions, leaving only four churches on the east side (*see* pp. 40, 50 & 81) and a tantalising group of houses at the south-west end which illustrates the quality of the loss. These houses are mainly Georgian, flat fronted, with sash windows, but among them are two much older buildings.

Reynolds & Sons, butchers, occupy No. 67, an exceptional double gabled early 17th-century house. It has typical top floor oriel windows on brackets, and a room with a large 16-light mullioned window on the first floor. Inside (accessible from the hotel), a contemporary ornamental plaster ceiling in two panels has eight different floral sprays in the corners including lilies, tulips, peas and pomegranates. This is a building of rare architectural distinction.

Next door is the *White Hart Hotel* with a history of great complexity. It probably dates from the 15th century or earlier, and reputedly belonged to the lawyer William Wynard who left it for the endowment of his almshouses (*see* p. 124). Constant change and renovation now make it difficult to assess what is genuine and what is bogus but despite that it is hard to resist the aura of antiquity. In the 18th century it was a coaching inn and the cobbled yard remains, now romantically wreathed in wisteria and obstructed by a white marble nymph sculpted in 1867 by B. Lombardi. To the right, in the lower bar, parts of the 15th-century house remain: a richly carved, panelled ceiling and a huge fireplace. The hotel reception area at the end of the yard is now disguised as a stable, in the Bethlehem tradition, quite logically in fact, for here were the original stables.

SOUTHERNHAY

With the loss of Bedford Circus in the Blitz, Southernhay remains as the most imposing of the Regency set pieces in Exeter, notwithstanding its own casualties in 1942 and subsequent inept rebuilding. It began as a tree-lined promenade on land owned by the Dukes of Bedford and it was the fifth duke who employed Mathew Nosworthy, as in his other Exeter speculations, to plan the houses in 1792. Several builders were involved, and East Southernhay, which was not completed until *c.* 1825, reflects the changing designs.

West Southernhay was planned as four terraces. Two survive, both with the end wings projecting, as do the centre four houses in the northern terrace. Each one is five storeys high, three bays wide and brick built with the same detail throughout: double arches to the ground-floor windows, Coade stone vermiculated voussoirs and portrait keystones (there are nine varieties) around the doors, a string course above and a cornice beneath the attic storey. Coade stone ornament can be seen on Nosworthy's other Exeter houses, but its inspiration was probably the duke's, whose Bedford Square houses in London, dating from 1775, have similar voussoirs.

In 1974, the two bomb-damaged terraces were rebuilt as Broadwalk House – a hopelessly insensitive attempt to emulate the originals, which ignores 18th-century proportion and detail. The result is preposterous, summed up by futile balconies which no one ever uses. A far more successful innovation is the first floor walkway to the rear of the old terraces which commands good views of the city walls and cathedral, but still mistakes are made. In 1989 yet another skin deep neo-Georgian monster has been built at the opposite end of the terraces evading any attempt to emulate the 18th-century architecture with a 20th-century solution. This block is to be a hotel, the architects are Marshman, Warren and Taylor.

East Southernhay includes more Nosworthy houses and also a three-storey stuccoed terrace fronted by a Doric colonnade. Simplicity is the key to this neo-classical building with variations only in the deployment of columns and the addition of pediments to emphasise the centre and ends of the group. At the other end of the road there are more obviously quirky details: the gothic glazed porch added to Nos. 38-39, which deserves restoration, and the extravagant barley-sugar downpipe at No. 40. Southernhay House, perhaps by Nosworthy, sports a colonnade and entablature. Richardson described the house as, 'Representative of the large type of middle-class town house built a century ago'. Like the rest of Southernhay it is now converted to offices and one wonders if any have surviving domestic fittings.

105. The Synagogue, Mary Arches Street.

THE SYNAGOGUE, MARY ARCHES STREET

Anonymous, difficult to find and usually locked, it is nevertheless worth the effort locating this little building which is one of only three synagogues in Devon and architecturally very interesting. It is the second to be built on the site, the first in 1763 filled the space now used by the present anterooms and lavatories. The second, dated 1835, moved the axis through 90 degrees and since then, with the exception of a new ceiling, has hardly changed.

The rendered exterior offers no clues to the building's purpose and only a pair of fluted Doric columns either side of the front door hints at something unusual. Inside, the high-galleried chamber is dominated by the ark at the east end. Corinthian columns on green marbled plinths each support an urn and above the entablature the Ten Commandments in Hebrew are surmounted by a scrolled broken pediment. The panelling of the gallery, reserved for ladies only, and other woodwork is stained and varnished and the columns stencilled in glowing tones of red and gold. Some seats have carved arms, perhaps re-used from the 18th-century building, while the flambeau light fittings on brass columns flank the president's desk. It is a pity such a richly-furnished interior is not more accessible.

TADDYFORDE, NEW NORTH ROAD

White-painted flat-roofed houses spawned by the brave new world of the International Style are not a common sight in Exeter, but the Taddyforde Estate is an exception with an eccentric history.

Its origins are respectably medieval, harking back to the days when this city suburb was a toad-frequented ford across a stream running down the Hoopern valley. So it remained until the late 19th century when a 'Unitarian wood craftsman' named Kent Kingdon built the improbably-gabled Taddyforde House here, ornamented with tall chimneys, carved barge-boarding, fanciful verandahs, a tower and a chapel. It is a glorious jumble that stylistically might be labelled Victorian Tudor freestyle.

In the early 20th century it was bought by a Miss Morrison who was the ideal owner for such a bizarre house. She was a racing driver, gambler, and owner of wolf hounds, but she lived beyond her means and sold up to Mr. Fulford, the estate agent, upon whose death the house was divided into two units and the garden partitioned for building plots. The new houses are seaside deco and seem to fit uncomfortably into the lush hillside planting. The front doors each provide access to four purpose-built flats, solidly fitted with oak floors, teak window surrounds, flush zebra wood doors and fitted cupboards. Unfortunately all but two have lost their parapets and several have unacceptable replacement windows.

TUCKER'S HALL, FORE STREET

Mainly because it is rarely open, partly because a visit involves a hill climb and perhaps because the word 'Tucker' is obscure, the Hall is Exeter's least-visited tourist attraction. It is however one of the few tangible reminders of medieval Exeter's national prominence in the wool trade which made it the fifth largest and wealthiest city in the country.

Local guidebooks usually equate the name 'Tucker' with 'Fuller', an equally recondite description for a cloth finisher, and this was originally their guild chapel, built shortly after 1471 when the land on which it stands was acquired. It was then a single lofty space with the wagon roof lit by tall, three-light windows, but after the Reformation it was secularised and divided horizontally. The upper hall became a meeting place for members of the guild and the lower became a school. The walls of the upper hall were painted with figurative scenes, but the remains of these were obscured in the 1630s when the present oak panelling was installed. The panels are divided by fluted pilasters beneath a carved strap-work frieze and a heavy guilloche cornice supported on brackets carved to represent grotesque masks and tools of the woollen trade. The fireplace was also fitted then – it bears the date 1638 – and the roof sealed over but leaving the carved bosses.

Between 1875-6 the hall underwent a thorough restoration, and, in the case of the exterior, over restoration when the present two storeys of curious round-headed windows were

106. Taddyforde, New North Road.

107. Tucker's Hall, Fore Street.

108. Tudor House, Tudor Street.

introduced. The interior, however, remained intact and, appropriately, is still used by the City Company of Weavers, Fullers and Shearmen.

THE TUDOR HOUSE, TUDOR STREET

The house probably is Tudor, although some argue that the large sun-dried bricks used in its construction are typical of the mid-15th century, whilst others rely on documentation which suggests an early 17th-century date. Never mind, the fact that such a picturesque building survives at all in the shadows of the ugliest post-war developments in Exeter is a miracle and due entirely to the efforts of one man, Bill Lovell.

Mr. Lovell bought the house for £700 in 1964 when it was an electrical repair shop and in desperate straits. Single-handed it took him 10 years to restore at a cost of some £60,000, entirely without grant aid. It was financial suicide and Mr. Lovell was eventually forced to sell, consoled, however, with a Civic Trust award and the satisfaction that he had saved a unique Exeter building.

Slate hung facades are common enough in Totnes or Ashburton; in Exeter this is a rare survivor of the type, and because the house is double fronted to the street there was plenty of scope for intricately-cut slates to form patterns on the front wall and the two pentice roofs. Even the wreathed armorials, references to previous owners, are partly made of slate, all restored by Mr. Lovell with slates from Delabole in Cornwall. He also rebuilt the bay windows with their diamond panes and the front door, using seasoned oak and an iron door handle, once a railway truck coupling ring.

The interior is much more of a puzzle. Basically the house is four storeyed, each floor once two rooms deep, a staircase to the rear and a single cellar with a well. Today a cobbled passage leads in from the front door but, aside from the stone flags on the ground floor, some of the timber work and the brick nogging, not much else of the original appears to survive. To comply with fire regulations, the spiral staircase has been rebuilt recently and the rear stables converted into a banqueting hall with modern living accommodation above. It is difficult to visualise how the house once looked now that most of the internal lathe and plaster has been removed, partition walls broken through and fitted carpets and sofas substituted. Nevertheless enough remains, particularly of the exterior, to justify all the expense and hard work lavished on its preservation.

109. Underground Passages, Princesshay.

THE UNDERGROUND PASSAGES, PRINCESSHAY

These are worth seeing if only to experience something unique in Britain – a medieval underground aqueduct. Tours lasting 20 minutes are organised during summer months, when the guide explains that similar systems exist in Riyadh and Jerusalem (he could add Istanbul), cities which need to conserve water during torrid summer weather. That problem hardly applies to Exeter where the labyrinthine passages were built for reasons of convenience and strategy, allowing water to be conducted from outside the city walls to within easy access of the citizens.

The aqueduct is first documented in 1226 when a spring was tapped at Mount Pleasant and water piped underground to the cathedral precinct. By the 14th century about three miles of tunnel had been dug, some of it 30 feet underground. Visitors now see only a small section but the route is satisfyingly claustrophobic and at one point negotiable only on hands and knees. Brick and later stone walls are bottle shaped in section, with here and there the remains of stone hatches in the roof through which buckets used to be lowered. It is a pity that the security of shops and banks above prevent the shafts being reopened and an unusual mole-like view of Exeter exposed.

THE UNIVERSITY, PRINCE OF WALES ROAD

Thanks to its comfortable situation in a 20th-century landscaped campus, the University seems isolated, both geographically and historically, from the city, but in fact its origins are both urban and Victorian. A School of Art had been established in Exeter in 1854 and a School of Science in 1863; the two combined under the new roof of the Royal Albert Memorial Museum (*see* p. 79) in 1868 and by 1900 had expanded into a University College offering external degrees from London University. In 1911 a massively dull neo-Georgian block by architects Tait and Harvey was built in Bradninch Place (now the Arts Centre) to house the embryonic university. Fortunately, this building also soon proved inadequate and even more fortunately the 120-acre Streatham Estate, north of the city, was purchased in 1922 to provide a new rural campus centred on Streatham Hall (now named Reed Hall after Alderman W. H. Reed who provided the purchase money).

The Hall had been built in 1867 for Richard Thornton West, a millionaire member of Exeter's richest merchant and ship-building family. The style he chose was an appropriately opulent Italianate, built with cream bricks by the architect himself, W. Moore, who managed to have his name emblazoned on the entrance facade. The house is reputed to contain more window glass, relative to its size, than any other in the country, but its abiding fame rests with 'the subtle charm of a very beautiful garden . . . necessarily a garden of terraces' whose layout survives although a large palm house has been demolished, as they usually are. The conservatory, shaped like a vast Nissen hut, was moved to the *Imperial Hotel* where it can still be seen (*see* p. 52). Robert Veitch of the famous Exeter family of nurserymen was responsible for the garden's design. Today Reed Hall is used as a staff club, but why the university dons have allowed the interior to be decorated and furnished to resemble a hospital waiting room is a mystery. Only the tiled entrance hall retains a whiff of its swashbuckling Victorian origins.

After the purchase of Streatham Hall, the University College expanded quickly, guided by two Devonian architects, Vincent Harris (1876-1971) of Plymouth and his assistant Sydney Greenslade (1866-1955) of Exeter. The key to the development was a new road built parallel to the Hoopern valley, inaugurated in 1927 by the College president, the Prince of Wales, which gave Harris the opportunity to devise a formal group of buildings marshalled along its north side. Like most grandiose schemes it was never completed, but the buildings that were illustrate the very high quality of Harris's neo-Georgian architecture. The first to be constructed, in 1931, was the Washington Singer Laboratories (named after its benefactor whose family fortune had been made in sewing machines), finished to a standard undreamt of by university bursars today. It is built of brick with stone slates, now beautifully weathered and meticulously detailed, alternating cobble and York paving stones, oak panelled doors, gilded armorial shields, lead downpipes and stone dressings round the windows. The style is 'Wrenaissance' and very impressive it looks, although it

110. The University, Washington Singer Laboratories.

111. The University, Hatherley Laboratories.

hides a purely functional interior. At the back is a vast bay window which was intended to light the hall, and the hillside beyond has been laboriously landscaped to create a mysterious space recalling a classical open-air theatre, but never used as such.

The next important building by Harris was the former Roborough Library (1938-40) named after Lord Roborough, a former university president. Its capacity was 130,000 volumes, a figure reached by 1966 when a new library to cope with the overflow was built nearby. Comparison between the two is instructive. The old library relies on a lucid triple-bay design built around a single galleried reading room. It is a plan adapted from the medieval great hall, but with a rusticated 18th-century style entrance. Sir William Holford's new library in contrast uses no historical references and now looks an awful muddle. Even the University's historian, B. W. Clapp, pronounced it 'less than perfect'.

Student halls of residence were Harris's other concern and he designed two in 1933. Lopes Hall for women was, originally, a large Victorian gothic villa dated 1866. It was bought by the University and Harris provided a brick Queen Anne-style extension with shaped gables in 1933. The new men's hall, Mardon, was built to the north overlooking the Exe valley and Dartmoor. It resembles an early 18th-century country house: tall chimney-stacks, a high slate roof punctuated with dormers and regular rows of sash widows. Inside was less luxurious as the rooms were shared and spartan.

After the war Harris persevered with his grand scheme for the symmetrical siting of buildings. Thanks to a bequest from Mrs. Heath, whose maiden name was Hatherley, the Hatherley Laboratories were built in 1948-52 to balance the Singer Laboratories. Unfortunately, post-war austerity seems to have affected the design which is a skimpy neo-Georgian; it only comes to life in a series of wings to the rear which have vast glazed window walls, 1970s fashion.

In 1955 the University received its charter and in 1958 Harris was given the opportunity to bring his association with the University to a triumphant conclusion by building the Mary Harris Memorial Chapel, which he had first designed in 1943. It is named after the architect's mother and was Harris's gift to the University. It is also the focal point to his overall plan, closing off a road intended as a processional way which aligns with the north tower of the cathedral across the valley. The exterior conveys an impression of simplicity and symmetry built to a very high standard (the paving bricks for example are unusually large and hand-made). Inside is the same: red tile and slate floors, a brick gallery, white-painted brick walls and clear window glass. It might have proved too austere but for the wooden ceiling which was painted by Thomas Monnington, P.R.A. (1902-76). Monnington was an admirer of Piero de la Francesca and using egg tempera he recreated Piero's pearly blue and pink colours in circular patterns symbolising the Creation above a Giottesque frieze. It achieves an astonishingly celestial effect which lifts this building to the level of a minor masterpiece. Appropriately, a memorial service to Harris was held here after his death in 1971 and in 1988 the chapel became a listed building, one of the first 19 post-war buildings in the country to be selected.

Harris's successor as consulting architect was Sir William, later Lord, Holford (1907-75), and with him came a decline in the quality of the University's buildings. He dismissed his predecessor's work as 'parade ground architecture' and embarked on disjointed designs for the arts building (Queen's Building, 1956-8) the administration block (Northcote House, 1960) with lead-panelled oriels, some supported on extraordinary rams' heads, and the Student Union building (Devonshire House), the dates 1958-60 proclaimed on a large stone slab. His firm later designed the Duryard halls of residence which mark the nadir in the University's architectural history.

During the buoyant 1960s other well-known architects made their contributions. Sir Basil Spence (1907-76) designed the blockbuster tower of the physics building and, at its feet, the

112. The University chapel.

brick wedge of the Newman Building lecture theatres. Neither compares with his earlier successes at Coventry Cathedral and Sussex University. Equally massive is the brick mathematics and geology building by Louis de Soissons (1890-1962). During the 1980s another building boom has produced the sports hall and a third library, both vast, but in architectural terms unremarkable.

Fortunately, most of this post-war development has respected the landscape and the few large houses that once enjoyed these elevated outskirts of the city. They are now part of the University, but still retain their pleasure gardens. The oldest is Duryard, presiding over an avenue of vast sequoia trees. It is a brick Queen Anne house with neo-Georgian wings and inside linen fold panelling apparently removed from the Guildhall. To the north is Thomas Hall, formerly Great Duryard (named after C. V. Thomas, a solicitor and benefactor), a house of similar date built by Sir Thomas Jefford, Lord Mayor 1687-8, who had been knighted 'for his ingenuity in dyeing a piece of cloth scarlet on one side and blue on the other'. In 1771 it was remodelled and in 1935 converted into a women's hall of residence. Today only a bolection-moulded fireplace remains of the earliest date, but one room decorated in the Adam style, a pretty staircase and enough mahogany doors also survive to make it an enviable place in which to live. The grounds are just as good, comprising a walled garden entered under a charming hooded doorway and a magnificent aboretum around the front lawn. On the east side of the campus are two more houses, Lopes Hall, already mentioned (*see* p. 119) and to the north, Hoopern House, an early 19th-century Greek classical villa built for Mr. E. P. Lyon. Below it is the Hoopern valley and a series of dammed ponds which is a deservedly popular place for walking. It is vital this hillside should not be subjected to the frightful excesses of red brick and purple pantiled executive dwellings which are now beginning to despoil the upper reaches of Pennsylvania Road, which is sylvan no more.

THE VICARS' COLLEGE, SOUTH STREET

The remains of the College are now so pathetically meagre that they even fail to merit an explanatory plaque. Furthermore, and for no apparent reason, the entrance to what was the hall is crudely barred by an iron rail. Within, only two deeply-splayed windows, each with a mullion, transom and evidence of tracery in the head, exist. Up until 1942 a 16th-century linenfold panelled interior survived, but bombs completed the devastation of the College, which had already lost the last of its houses in 1893 and had been deprived of its charter in 1933.

The College had been founded in 1401 and comprised a street with gabled houses and gardens either side, a gatehouse, the hall, a buttery and kitchen, a library and a prebendal house. The extent of Exeter's loss can be gauged by comparison with the Vicars' Close at Wells, which survives intact, the houses still inhabited.

Reconstructed within the hall is an unremarkable stone doorway. It was originally part of the wall of a Saxon church built on the opposite side of South Street and absorbed into the medieval church of St George – demolished in 1843.

THE WALLS

Whereas the cathedral cities of York and Chester are dominated by their medieval walls, both offering elevated perambulations, one could be forgiven for missing Exeter's walls entirely. And yet, hidden behind buildings and trees and sometimes buttressing existing roads, about three-quarters of the walls' original 2,600 yards' length survives.

They began as an earth rampart thrown up in about A.D. 120 by the Romans on a typical rectangular plan with a gate on each side. Thereafter they were repeatedly strengthened with masonry additions using Pocombe and Thorverton stone, but Roman ashlar, neater than medieval courses, can still be seen in Post Office Street (largely rebuilt during the 17th century), Southernhay West, Northernhay Gardens and from South Street to the river. In places, particularly in Northernhay, the medieval wall soars over 25 feet high and there are still substantial remains of the watergate at Quay Lane and barbicans at Northernhay, known as Athelstan's Tower, and Trinity Green. Lollard's Tower near the latter was rebuilt in 1912 and is reputedly the place where heretics were imprisoned before being burned at the stake in Southernhay.

The walls saw action many times, most recently during the Civil War, when the city was twice besieged, but by the late 17th century they were obsolete and Daniel Defoe mistakenly believed in 1714, 'The walls and all the old works are demolished'. In fact, the four monstrous medieval gates were not finally demolished for another 100 years: the north in 1769, the east in 1784, the west in 1815, and the south, by then a notorious prison, in 1819. The lock and key to the west gate is now in the Royal Albert Memorial Museum and the site of each merely commemorated by a bronze plaque. More recent demolitions occurred in the 1950s to make way for new roads in Southernhay, the Friars and Princesshay.

113. Vicars' College, South Street.

114. The Walls, Northernhay.

Early this century some restoration was carried out and efforts were made in 1977 to mark the walls' course, but far more could be done to publicise what is, after all, Exeter's oldest and largest monument. Certainly a properly marked walk around its entire length is long overdue.

WEST STREET

It says a lot for medieval carpentry that in 1961 a 500-year-old timber-framed house, after years of neglect, was successfully moved 50 yards on rollers, out of the path of the new ring road into West Street. It is now well known as 'The House that Moved' but conveniently forgotten is 48-49 West Street, the house that previously occupied this site. Ironically, it resembled its successor in dating from the 15th century and having two jettied storeys. It was offered to Exeter City Council for £100 in 1941 but the offer was rejected and the house demolished for a road-widening scheme that never happened. The site remained vacant for the next 20 years.

Also forgotten is the major overhaul applied to 'The House that Moved' after it was re-sited. It convincingly resembles a 15th-century merchant's house but in fact only the structural timbers and three traceried windows are original, the rest: ground floor windows, infill panels and roof are all new. Initially a shop and kitchen filled the ground floor; above it hefty oak jettying and corner dragon beams, over a foot square, supported the hall and

115. West Street: on the left, The House that Moved.

buttery. Above that perched the solar on more jettying, amounting to a total oversail of two feet, eight inches. A gabled cockloft completed the ensemble. Hoskins considered it the best surviving old merchant's house in Exeter.

West Street was planned as a main route from the Quay to the city via the West Gate. Today it is a minor one-way street; the gate was demolished in 1815 and is remembered today only by a bronze plaque. Across the road is a more picturesque cobbled relic, Stepcote Hill, and on the corner another ostensibly 15th-century merchant's house of four storeys, this time with Heavitree stone ground floor. Its chequered timberwork and irregular angles appear venerable enough, but in fact it is substantially restored although not so much as its next door neighbour. Stepcote Hill itself was another main road to the city but now is only a shadow of its former self. None of the tall gabled medieval houses that lined both sides, even as late as the 19th century, survives and it is relegated to a minor tourist attraction.

WONFORD HOSPITAL, DRYDEN ROAD

In contrast to the popular 18th-century view that mentally ill patients were figures of fun, the Victorians tackled the problem of their treatment with more sensitivity and typical thoroughness, beginning with the Lunacy Act of 1845 and later, in Exeter, the erection of three vast mental hospitals. Of these, the oldest is Wonford, built in 1866, to the design of a local architect, W. E. Cross. His choice of style was a florid Jacobethan intending to impart a domestic rather that institutional character, so that the 70 private patients would feel they were in familiar surroundings despite the palatial scale.

The approach to the hospital is bordered by walls overhung by a canopy of ilex trees, part of the 72 acres of landscaping planned by John Veitch, whose Exeter firm enjoyed a national reputation. A lodge in the same baronial style and a fir tree avenue presage the long symmetrical facade, buttressed and gabled with corner towers, each end surmounted by fanciful ironwork crowns. It is built of a bluish limestone from Westleigh near Tiverton, the openings dressed in Bath stone.

Entrance is via a balustraded porch into the staircase hall where there is more ornate ironwork in the balusters and brackets of the lantern. Corridors lead off either side to the patients' quarters, and originally the dining, drawing, music and billiards rooms, plus, in 1912, a lounge and ballroom. There is a small gothic chapel to the rear.

The contrast between this stylish Victorian building and the brutal concrete hulk of the 20th-century Royal Devon and Exeter Hospital built in Wonford's grounds in 1968-71 (architect: Watkins Grey), could not be greater and it is ironic that the latter is already scheduled for demolition, to be rebuilt in the 1990s at a cost of £64,000,000. In comparison, the cost of building Wonford Hospital in 1869 was a mere £35,000.

WYNARD'S ALMSHOUSES, MAGDALEN STREET

Old buildings may need adapting to new uses if they are to survive, and there was no better solution for these almshouses, with their long tradition of community service, than to become an advice centre in 1972.

They date from the 1430s when William Wynard, a Recorder of Exeter, established them, together with the Trinity Chapel, for the benefit of 12 infirm old people. Conversion by Vinton Hall, the City architect, was carefully done so that today, when passing under the entrance arch and leaving the busy ring road behind, there is a sensation of slipping back a few centuries. Venerable Heavitree stone walls surround an attractive cobbled yard shaded by an ilex. A well-house survives which once served the inhabitants whose individual houses each have oak front doors and dormer windows in the tiled roof. In fact what one sees is largely a Victorian restoration.

116. Wonford Hospital, Dryden Road.

117. Wynard's Almshouses, Magdalen Street.

By the end of the 18th century ownership of the almshouses had passed to the Kennaway family and it was George Kennaway who rebuilt them in the 1860s with the aid of the diocesan architect, Edward Ashworth, and the sculptor, Harry Hems. In particular the chapel, which had become the family mausoleum, was thoroughly restored and redecorated with impressive results. It is a small building entered under a gallery which retains its 15th-century carved parapet. The nave, with pews arranged in collegiate fashion, is separated from the chancel by a richly-carved arch which is also a 15th-century survivor, but the chancel itself is thoroughly Victorianised. Stained glass by Hardman of Birmingham vies with green and gold stencilling, polychromed tiles on the walls and gilded bosses in the arch braced roof. It is a most unexpected treat and the author of it is immortalised in a full length brass set in the tiled floor, shown holding a model of his creation. Incredibly this delightful building, designed for peace and contemplation, is hardly used by the caring organisations that fill the offices around it. It is a terrible waste and it should be tidied up and put back into use – now.

Glossary

Acroterion: A decorative feature at the apex of a **gable** or **pediment**.
Adam Style: The elegant architectural style introduced by the Adam brothers to Britain in the late 18th century, based on the Roman antique.
Aisle: The part of a church built parallel to the **nave**.
Ambulatory: The part of a church built around the back of an altar.
Apse: A semicircular or multiangular end to a **chancel** or chapel.
Arcade: A row of arches carried on **piers** or columns.
Arch Brace: A curved timber arch that spans a roof below the level of a **collar beam**.
Architrave: The moulded frame to an opening.

Bailey: An enclosure behind castle walls.
Baldacchino: A canopy over an altar.
Barge-board: A board, sometimes carved, fitted to the edge of a **gable** end.
Baroque: An exuberant development of **classical architecture** during the 17th and early 18th centuries.
Barrel Vault: A continuously arched roof with a semi-circular section.
Basilica: A church divided into a **nave** with a **clerestory** and lower **aisles** on each side.
Bolection Moulding: A projecting moulding used as a frame to a panel, door etc.
Boss: A carved block usually at the intersection of a **rib vault**.
Buttery: A storeroom for food or drink in a medieval house.
Buttress: A thickening of a stone or brick wall to provide additional support.

Capital: The crowning feature at the top of a column or **pilaster**.
Casement Window: An outward opening window hinged on one side.
Castellated: Battlemented.
Cellarium: A monastic storehouse.
Chamfer: The surface created by cutting away a sharp edge, usually at 45 degrees to the other two surfaces.
Chancel: The east end of a church in which the high altar stands.
Chapter House: The place of assembly in a monastic church, adjoining the **cloisters**.
Classical Architecture: Greek and Roman architecture on which many subsequent styles of architecture were based.
Clerestory: The glazed upper storey in a church **nave**.
Cloister: A quadrangle surrounded by arcaded passages connecting the domestic areas of a monastery with the abbey church.
Coade Stone: An artificial stone manufactured by the London firm of Coade and Seely used for architectural ornament during the late 18th and 19th centuries.
Cockloft: An attic room.
Collarbeam: A **tie-beam** connecting each side of a roof, usually more than halfway up the roof slope.
Colonnette: A small column.
Corbel: A block projecting from a wall that provides support.
Corinthian Order: The most elaborate of the classical architectural orders with the **capital** carved to represent formalised acanthus leaves.
Cornice: Ornamental moulding at the top edge of a wall.
Coving: A large concave moulding.
Crocket: A projecting decorative feature in **gothic architecture** carved in leaf form.
Crow Steps: Small steps built up the side of a **gable**.
Cupola: A small domed turret.
Curtain Wall: A connecting wall between castle towers.
Cusp: The point formed where **tracery** foils meet.

Dado: The lower part of a wall.
Decorated Architecture: The style of English **gothic architecture** built between *c.* 1290 and 1350.
Diaper: Surface decoration with a repetitive pattern.
Doric Order: The first of the orders in Greek **classical architecture**.
Dragon Beam: A weight bearing beam projecting diagonally from the corner of a building.
Drip Mould: A projecting moulding, above an opening, intended to throw off water.

Egg and Dart: Decoration comprising a formalised pattern of alternating ovals and arrow heads.
Entablature: The entire horizontal part of an **order** supported by columns or **pilasters**.

Fanlight: A window over a door, often semicircular in shape.
Flemish Bond: Bricks laid in courses of alternating headers and stretchers.
Fluting: Parallel grooves running vertically up a column or **pilaster**.

Gable: The triangular upper part of a wall at the end of a pitched roof.
Garderobe: The medieval term for a closet.
Gargoyle: A projecting water spout carved in grotesque form.
Gothic Architecture: The style of European ecclesiastical architecture first built in France during the mid-12th century and revived in Britain during the late 18th and early 19th centuries.
Greek Revival Architecture: The unadorned style of classical Greek temples revived in the early 19th century.
Guilloche: A pattern of interlacing ornament used to enrich mouldings.

Hammer Beam: A horizontal beam projecting at wall plate level supporting a vertical timber (hammer post) and brace beneath a **collar beam**.
Hipped Gable: A **gable**, the top of which is part of the roof.

Iconostasis: A screen supporting icons and separating the sanctuary from the **nave** in the Orthodox Church.
International Style: The term used to describe the new architecture of the 20th century developed on the continent and in the U.S.A. during the 1920s.
Ionic Order: The most elegant of the classical architectural orders exemplified by the scrolled **capital** and the fluted column.

Jamb: The straight side of a door or window.
Jetty: The projection formed by the oversailing of an upper storey over the one below in a timber-framed building.
Joggle: The shaping of stone blocks with a notch and corresponding projection to prevent slipping of adjacent masonry.

Keep: A castle stronghold.
Keystone: The centre wedge-shaped stone in an arch.
King Post: An upright timber connecting a **tie beam** to a **collar beam**.

Lancet Window: A narrow, pointed arched window.
Linenfold: Panelling representing formalised linen folds.
Lintel: A horizontal beam bridging an opening.
Long and Short Work: Anglo-Saxon **quoins** comprising long stones set vertically and horizontally alternately.

Mansard: A roof with each face having two slopes, the lower being steeper.
Modillion: One of a series of small ornamental brackets below a **cornice** in **classical architecture**.
Mullion: A vertical member dividing a window into more than one light.
Muntin: The vertical timber member dividing panelling in a door or screen.

Narthex: A large enclosed porch at the entrance to a church.
Nave: The central body of a church extending from west door to **chancel**.
Neo-Classical Architecture: The austere reaction to **baroque** architecture during the late 18th and early 19th centuries representing a return to established classical principles.
Newel: A central post in a winding staircase, or the end post in a flight of stairs.
Nogging: Infill between timber framework.

Oculus: A circular opening.
Ogee: A pointed arch with a double curve each side.
Order: In **classical architecture** a column with a base, shaft and **capital**.
Oriel: A projecting window on an upper floor.
Ovolo: A small convex moulding.

Palladian Architecture: The English interpretation of Renaissance architecture based on the designs of the 16th-century Italian architect, Palladio.
Patera: A circular ornament in low relief.
Pediment: The triangular **gable** end above a **portico** used in **classical architecture**.
Pentice: A projecting roof providing shelter.
Perpendicular Style: The style of English **gothic architecture** built during the period *c.* 1350-1530.
Piano Nobile: The principal floor of a house with reception rooms, usually over a basement.
Pier: A solid masonry support.
Pilaster: The shallow section of a column attached to a wall.
Plat Band: A broad undecorated **string course**.
Porte Cochère: a carriage porch.
Portico: An imposing porch to a classical building usually supported on columns and surmounted by a **pediment**.
Pulpitum: A stone screen in a church dividing **nave** from **chancel**.
Putto: A statue of a small naked boy.

Quatrefoil: Circular **tracery** divided into four equal lobed parts.
Quoins: Bricks or stones, often emphasised, forming the angles of a building.

Reredos: An ornamental screen behind an altar.
Rib Vault: A roof vault divided up by diagonal ribs.
Romanesque Architecture: The European style of architecture current from the 9th to the 12th centuries typified by the round-headed arch and massive walls.
Rood: A cross or crucifix.
Roof Truss: The principal supporting member in a timber-framed roof.

Sash Window: A double-hung window opened by sliding up or down.
Scallop Capital: A **capital** carved as if pleated on each side.
Screens Passage: A screened passage separating the great hall of a medieval house from the kitchen and service rooms.
Shaped Gable: A gable with one or more curves in its elevation.
Soffit: The underside of an opening or section of ceiling.
Solar: The upper living room in a medieval house.
Spandrel: The triangular space enclosed between the curved top of an arch and its rectangular surround.
Stiff Leaf Capital: A **capital** carved with rigidly stylised foliage, common in the late 12th to early 13th centuries.
Strapwork: Decoration comprising interlaced shapes, resembling fretwork or leather, common in Elizabethan and Jacobean England.
String Course: A horizontal moulding along the face of a wall.
Stucco: External render on a building.

Terrazzo: A floor finished with a decorative pattern of marble chips.
Tie Beam: A horizontal beam in a pitched roof usually connecting the walls at wall plate level.
Tierceron Vault: A stone vault with secondary ribs meeting at the ridge.
Tracery: Ornamental ribs in the upper part of a window or covering a blank arch or vault.
Transept: The parts of a cruciform plan church projecting at right angles to the main building.
Transom: A horizontal member dividing a window or panel.
Triforium: An arcaded wall passage in a church above main **arcade** level.
Tuck Pointing: Thin, incised lines of usually white lime putty set into thicker mortar joints in brickwork.
Tuscan Order: The earliest and plainest of the Roman classical architectural orders.

Venetian Window: A window with three lights, the centre one arched and larger than the two flanking it.
Vermiculation: Masonry carved with worm-like channels over its surface.
Voussoir: A wedge-shaped block used in the construction of an arch.

Wagon Roof: A semi-circular vault.
Wainscot: Timber lining to walls.
Waterleaf Capital: A **capital** carved in formalised leaf shape, introduced in the later 12th century.

Detail from the Guildhall

Select Bibliography

Barber, Chips, *The Lost City of Exeter*, Exeter 1982.
Bennett, Leigh, *Historic Exeter*, Exeter 1940.
Bidwell, Paul, *The Legionary Bathhouse & Basilica & Forum at Exeter*, Exeter 1979.
Bishop, Herbert and Prideaux, Edith, *The Building of the Cathedral Church of St Peter in Exeter*, Exeter 1922.
Brockett, Allan, *Nonconformity in Exeter 1650-1875*, Exeter 1962.
— *Witnesses, a History of the Six Members of the Exeter Council of Congregational Churches*, Dawlish 1962.
Chanter, J. F., *The Bishop's Palace and its Story*, London 1932.
— *The Custos & College of the Vicars Choral of the Choir of the Cathedral Church of St Peter, Exeter*, Exeter 1933.
Chitty, Michael, *Industrial Archaeology of Exeter*, Exeter 1974.
Clapp, B. W., *The University of Exeter. A History*, Exeter 1982.
Colvin, Howard, *A Biographical Dictionary of British Architects 1600-1840*, London 1978.
Cossins, James, *Reminiscences of Exeter 50 Years Since*, Exeter 1878.
Cresswell, Beatrix, *Exeter Churches.* Exeter 1908.
Crocker, James, *Sketches of Old Exeter*, London 1879.
Defoe, Daniel, *A Tour through England and Wales*, London 1948; first published 1724-6.
Devon County Council, *Devon's Heritage Buildings & Landscape*, Exeter 1982.
Falla, Trevor, *Discovering Exeter, Heavitree*, Exeter 1983.
Fiennes, Celia, *The Illustrated Journeys of Celia Fiennes 1685-1712*, Exeter 1982.
Fox, Lady Aileen, *Roman Exeter*, Manchester 1952.
Freeman, Edward and Hunt, William, *Historic Towns, Exeter*, London 1887.
Greenaway, Joyce, *Discovering Exeter, St David's*, Exeter 1981.
Greenslade, Robert, 'Almshouses of Exeter & Tiverton', unpublished thesis, Manchester University 1954.
Gunnis, Rupert, *Dictionary of British Sculptors 1660-1851*, London 1951.
Hardy, Paul, *Exeter – Profile of a City*, Bristol 1982.
Harris, J. Delpratt, *The Royal Devon & Exeter Hospital*, Exeter 1922.
Harvey, Hazel, *Discovering Exeter, Pennsylvania*, Exeter 1984.
— *Discovering Exeter, Sidwell Street*, Exeter 1986.
Harvey, John, *English Mediaeval Architects*, London 1954.
Hoskins, W. G., *Two Thousand Years in Exeter*, Chichester 1960.
Jenkins, Alexander, *The History and Description of the City of Exeter*, 2nd edn., Exeter 1841.
Lega-Weekes, Ethel, *Some Studies in the Topography of the Cathedral Close, Exeter*, Exeter 1915.
Little, Bryan, *Exeter*, London 1953.
MacKay, Keith and others, *Exeter School 1880-1983*, Exeter 1984.
Maggs, Colin, *Rail Centres: Exeter*, Shepperton 1985.
Newton, Robert, *Victorian Exeter*, Leicester 1968.
— *Eighteenth Century Exeter*, Exeter 1984.
Oliver, George, *The History of Exeter*, London 1861.
Parry, H. Lloyd and Brakspear, Sir Harold, *St Nicholas Priory*, Exeter 1946.
Pevsner, Sir Nikolaus, *The Buildings of England, South Devon*, Harmondsworth 1952.
— *A History of Building Types*, London 1976.
Pevsner, Sir Nikolaus and Cherry, Bridget, *The Buildings of England, Devon*, 2nd edn., London 1989
Portman, D., *Exeter Houses 1400-1700*, Exeter 1966.
Richardson, A. E. and Gill, C. L., *Regional Architecture in the West of England*, London 1924.
Russell, P. M. G., *A History of the Exeter Hospitals 1170-1948*, Exeter 1976.
Ryton, John, *Banks & Banknotes of Exeter 1769-1906*, Exeter 1984.
Sinar, Miss, *The Castle of Exeter*, Exeter 1956.
Shapter, Thomas, *The History of Cholera in Exeter.* London 1849.
Sharp, Thomas, *Exeter Phoenix*, London 1946.

Simpson, M. A. and Lloyd, T. H., *Middle Class Housing in Britain*, Newton Abbot 1977.
Thomas, Peter and Warren, Jacqueline, *Aspects of Exeter*, Plymouth 1980.
Thomas, Peter, *Exeter in Old Picture Postcards*, Zaltbommel 1983.
Venn, Gilbert, *Discovering Exeter, St Leonards*, Exeter 1982.
Venning, Norman, *Exeter, the Blitz and Rebirth of the City*. Exeter 1988.
Vowell, John, alias Hoker, *The Description of the City of Exeter c. 1580*, edited for the Devon & Cornwall Record Society, Exeter 1947.
Ward & Lock, *A Pictorial and Descriptive Guide to Exeter and South Devon*, London n.d.
White, John, 'Provincialism: A Study of the Work of the General Practitioner Architects of Georgian Exeter, 1760-1840', unpublished thesis, Manchester University 1963.
Wood, Margaret, *The English Mediaeval House*, London 1981.
Worrall, Geoffrey, *Target Exeter*, Exeter 1979.
Worth & Co., *Exeter Guide Book*, 4th edn., Exeter 1905.
Worthy, Charles, *The History of the Suburbs of Exeter*, Plymouth 1892.
Youings, Joyce, *Tuckers Hall, Exeter*, Exeter 1968.

PERIODICALS

The Builder
Devon and Cornwall Notes and Queries
Devon Life
Exeter Museum Archaeological Field Unit – *Archaeology in Exeter*
Exeter Flying Post
Transactions of the Devonshire Association
Transactions of the Exeter Diocesan Architectural Society

Index

A page number in **bold** denotes an illustration

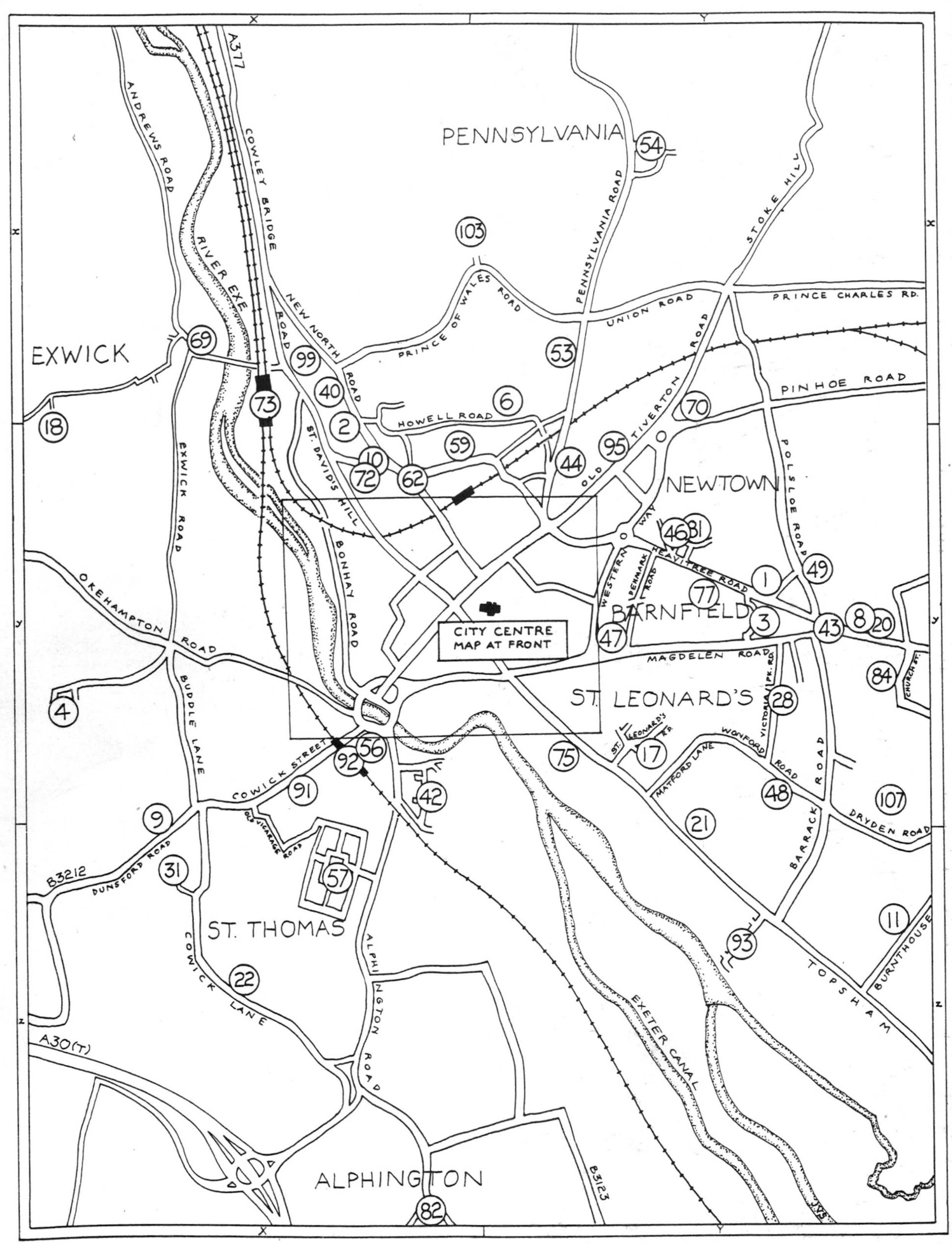

PENNSYLVANIA
EXWICK
NEWTOWN
BARNFIELD
ST. LEONARD'S
ST. THOMAS
ALPHINGTON
CITY CENTRE
MAP AT FRONT
A377
COWLEY BRIDGE ROAD
ANDREWS ROAD
RIVER EXE
NEW NORTH ROAD
PRINCE OF WALES ROAD
PENNSYLVANIA ROAD
STOKE HILL
UNION ROAD
PRINCE CHARLES RD.
TIVERTON ROAD
OLD TIVERTON ROAD
PINHOE ROAD
HOWELL ROAD
ST. DAVID'S HILL
BONHAY ROAD
EXWICK ROAD
OKEHAMPTON ROAD
BUDDLE LANE
WESTERN WAY
PENNARK ROAD
HEAVITREE ROAD
POLSLOE ROAD
MAGDELEN ROAD
VICTORIA PK. RD
CHURCH ST.
ST. LEONARD'S RD.
WONFORD ROAD
MATFORD LANE
BARRACK ROAD
DRYDEN ROAD
COWICK STREET
OLD VICARAGE ROAD
DUNSFORD ROAD
B3212
COWICK LANE
ALPHINGTON ROAD
EXETER CANAL
TOPSHAM
BURNTHOUSE
A30(T)
B3123